A Light to the West

BOOKS BY SWAMI PRABHAVANANDA

Original Works

THE SERMON ON THE MOUNT ACCORDING TO VEDANTA

RELIGION IN PRACTICE

YOGA AND MYSTICISM

THE SPIRITUAL HERITAGE OF INDIA
   (with Frederick Manchester)

VEDIC RELIGION AND PHILOSOPHY

Translations

SRIMAD BHAGAVATAM: THE WISDOM OF GOD

SHANKARA'S CREST-JEWEL OF DISCRIMINATION
   (with Christopher Isherwood)

THE UPANISHADS: BREATH OF THE ETERNAL
   (with Frederick Manchester)

THE SONG OF GOD: BHAGAVAD GITA
   (with Christopher Isherwood)

HOW TO KNOW GOD: THE YOGA APHORISMS OF PATANJALI
   (with Christopher Isherwood)

SWAMI PREMANANDA: TEACHINGS AND REMINISCENCES

NARADA'S WAY OF DIVINE LOVE

A Light
to the West

The Life and Teachings of
Swami Prabhavananda

by
Pravrajika Anandaprana

VEDANTA PRESS
Hollywood, California

Vedanta Society of Southern California
1946 Vedanta Place
Hollywood, California 90068-3996

FOR MORE INFORMATION

To learn in greater detail about the teachings in this book,
please email **info@vedanta.org** or write to:

VEDANTA SOCIETY
1946 Vedanta Place
Hollywood, CA 90068-3996
Vedanta Society 323-465-7114
Vedanta Catalog 800-816-2242

For information on our books: **www.vedanta.com**
For information about Vedanta: **www.vedanta.org**

Library of Congress Cataloging-in-Publication Data

Names: Anandaprana, Pravrajika, 1922-2014, author. I Brahmaprana, Pravrajika, editor.
Title: A light to the West: the life and teachings of Swami Prabhavananda /
by Pravrajika Anandaprana; edited by Pravrajika Brahmaprana.
Description: Hollywood: Vedanta Society of Southern California, 2016. I
Description based on print version record and CIP data provided by
publisher; resource not viewed.
Identifiers: LCCN 2016020933 (print) I LCCN 2016010097 (ebook) I ISBN
9780874817317 (kindle) I ISBN 9780874813395 (pbk. : alk. paper)
Subjects: LCSH: Prabhavananda, Swami, 1893-1976. I Gurus—United
States—Biography. I Vedanta.
Classification: LCC BL1175.P675 (print) I LCC BL1175.P675 A63 2016 (ebook) I
DDC 294.5092 [B] —dc23
LC record available at https://lccn.loc.gov/2016020933

Cover Design: Michael Hogue and Kevin Goodbar
Illustrations: Vedanta Society of Southern California Archives

PHONES PBX : (033)
2654-1144   2654-5700
2654-1180   2654-5701
2654-5391   2654-5702
2654-9581   2654-5703
2654-9681   2654-8494
FAX   : 033-2654-4071
E-Mail : president@belurmath.org
          presidentoffice@belurmath.org

RAMAKRISHNA MATH

P.O. BELUR MATH, DIST. HOWRAH

WEST BENGAL : 711 202

INDIA

Shri Ramakrishna Sharanam

MESSAGE

I am glad to know that a book on the life and teachings of Swami Prabhavanandaji, entitled *A Light to the West*, is being published by the Vedanta Society of Southern California, Hollywood.

Swami Prabhavanandaji Maharaj had the rare opportunity to have intimate association with his guru, Swami Brahmanandaji Maharaj, and other direct disciples of Sri Ramakrishna. It was also his great fortune to meet Sri Sarada Devi, the Holy Mother.

Swami Prabhavananda was indeed a great soul in whom saintly qualities manifested. He not only founded the Vedanta Society in Hollywood but was also a scholar, fine writer, versatile conversationalist, and a successful spiritual emissary of Vedanta in the West. He attracted to the Ramakrishna movement such renowned Western scholars and writers as Aldous Huxley, Christopher Isherwood, Gerald Heard, among others, as well as renowned Hollywood cinema artists. With the help of literary luminaries, Swami Prabhavanandaji published many spiritual books in English and, in this way, enriched the Ramakrishna movement in the West.

That this book may enlighten the reader with thoughts of spirituality is my earnest prayer!

(Swami Atmasthananda)

President

Ramakrishna Math & Ramakrishna Mission

Contents

Illustrations

Editor's Preface

SHORTLY AFTER SWAMI Prabhavananda's passing on July 4, 1976, Pravrajika Anandaprana, his personal secretary, collected his reminiscences and her own notes of his teachings and arranged them as a biographical narrative, entitled *A Historical Record: from Conversations with Swami Prabhavananda.* In the fall of 1987, Anandaprana had this printed privately in a limited edition in order to share these precious memories with a small number of intimate devotees.

In 2013 Wick Allison, a student of Vedanta from Dallas, went on retreat at the Ramakrishna Monastery in Trabuco Canyon. In the monastery library he discovered Anandaprana's manuscript and offered to publish it. In the course of editing, the original manuscript underwent some expansion with the inclusion of additional material along with editorial clarifications and corrections. This was all accomplished with Anandaprana's permission and approval and later in accordance with her expressed wishes.

In 2014 Swami Sarvadevananda, head of the Vedanta Society of Southern California, requested from the General Secretary of the Ramakrishna Order, Swami Suhitananda, special permission to publish Anandaprana's book. Permission was granted by the trustees of the order on October 15, 2014, just two months before Anandaprana's passing on December 29, 2014.

We are indebted not only to Swamis Suhitananda and Sarvadevananda but also to Wick Allison for having spearheaded this project. Wick has lent invaluable editorial and technical expertise as well as assistance in the beautiful cover design.

I am deeply grateful to Pravrajika Anandaprana and Swami Sarvadevananda for entrusting me with the task of preparing this book for publication and for Swami Sarvadevananda's helpful suggestions and support. I am also grateful to Devadatta Kali for his insightful and conscientious contribution in editing the text and to Pravrajika Vrajaprana for her valuable input. I also wish to thank Swami Vimalatmananda, secretary to revered Swami Atmasthananda, and Gopal Stavig for research that corroborates historical details mentioned in this book. Finally, I would like to acknowledge the important role of Swami Vedamritananda at the Vedanta Press for bringing this book to fruition.

Guru Purnima, 2016   Pravrajika Brahmaprana

Preface

THIS VOLUME IS composed of notes taken over the years of conversations with Swami Prabhavananda, the guiding light of the Vedanta movement in Southern California for more than four decades. Not only do these conversations provide a background for the early history of the Vedanta Society of Southern California and its spiritual heritage within the Ramakrishna tradition, they also provide a personal biography and reveal the loving character of an inspired teacher.

Great teachers attract devoted students, who are likely to venerate their teacher. Whenever Swami Prabhavananda encountered overly zealous guru worship, he would say, "Sri Ramakrishna, Holy Mother, Swamiji [Swami Vivekananda], and Maharaj [Swami Brahmananda]—these are our Four-Square Gospel. These are to be worshiped." Swami Prabhavananda considered himself only "second in command" as an instrument for a message imbued deeply in his heart, the life-giving words of Sri Ramakrishna as he received them through Swami Brahmananda and other direct disciples. It is hoped that you will find the conversations and reminiscences contained in this book personally meaningful.

Editorial clarifications inserted within quoted material are marked by square brackets.

Durga Puja, 1987   Pravrajika Anandaprana
Santa Barbara

Part One: Life

CHAPTER ONE

The Early Years

THE FUTURE SWAMI Prabhavananda was born Abani Ghosh in Surmanagar, a village three miles from Vishnupur in West Bengal, on December 26, 1893. He shared his premonastic name, Ghosh, with Swamis Brahmananda, Premananda, and Subodhananda, as he pointed out happily in later years.

Swami Prabhavananda's mother, Jnanada Sarkar, was very devout. She performed worship regularly and would sometimes tell Swami that this god or that goddess had visited her in her dreams. Swami would exclaim, "Mother, what are you saying!" He thought her claims preposterous.

Jnanada was the favorite daughter of Ishwar Sarkar, Swami's grandfather. Ishwar, a lawyer, once represented a client in a case in which Gadadhar Chattopadhyay of Kamarpurkur, the young Ramakrishna, was to be called as a witness.* Gadadhar came to Vishnupur one day, stood on the porch of Ishwar's house, and told Swami's grandfather, "If I am called as a witness, I will tell the whole truth."

We do not know what the lawsuit was about or why the future Sri Ramakrishna would be called as a witness, but we do know that Ishwar thereafter arranged for the two parties to settle out of court.† He said about Ramakrishna: "We knew him then as "Mad Gadai."

Ishwar Sarkar's family deity was Shiva. Every morning a servant would bring Ishwar a certain box. Ishwar used to write

---

* Ramakrishna was born Gadadhar Chattopadhyay in 1836.
† For details of the court case, see Swami Saradananda, *Sri Ramakrishna: the Great Master*, Section IV.4.18.

108 times "Jaya Sri Durga," fold the paper with the Mother's name and put it into the box before he started his work. The porch of his home served as his law office. He used to sit there and tell his beads, stopping the *japa* [meditative repetition of a mantra] when clients came to talk to him.

Swami Prabhavananda said about his maternal grandfather, "He was a devotee in a way, but we made fun of him." Ishwar used to cry while watching religious plays. On such occasions Swami used to tease his grandfather, saying, "Grandpa, have you put chilies under your eyes?" During the long theatrical performances, Swami and the other young children present would become bored and fall asleep. "But," Swami remembered, "whenever Hanuman came on the stage we would wake up."

Swami's father was Kumud Behari Ghosh. When asked what his father was like, Swami said, "He was very tenderhearted and charitable in his way. He would make big money, say 400 rupees per day. When he died, there was nothing left.* In our home, where my father lived, there was cooking in one place for the family and cooking in another place for anybody who would come—a separate kitchen and quantity of food every day. My father did this; not everybody did this. People knew about it, so they would come.

"He was a very ethical man. He was a lawyer, but he would not represent anyone in matters involving falsehood."

A personal tragedy brought Kumud Ghosh into the Sarkar family and determined his choice of wife and profession. Kumud's parents were worshipers of Vishnu and one year went on a pilgrimage to Puri. There they died of cholera, leaving two young sons as orphans. One of the orphaned boys was Kumud. Kumud's father had been a zamindar, a landowner.

Ishwar Sarkar, Swami's maternal grandfather, was the lawyer of the estate left by Kumud's father. Ishwar took Kumud into his own home and educated him to become a lawyer too. When Kumud was still very young, Ishwar married him to young Jnanada, the oldest of his five daughters.

---

* He died about 1916, two years after Swami joined the monastery.

Swami told us incidents from his youth:

"When I was a little boy, I had a fight with another boy. I got him down on the ground and then kicked him. My mother came running and said, "What are you doing! Don't you know that you should not kick anyone, because God dwells in him?' To those of us brought up in the Vedanta tradition in India, the question of where to find God does not even arise, because from our very childhood we are taught that the kingdom of God is within us.

"Once I got mad at my mother and another relative. So I stayed outdoors and hid somewhere. I would not come in. My parents pretended to ignore me. After some time I wrote on our gate, 'Call me once more and I'll come.' But I was completely ignored, and so I came out of hiding.

"Once when I was very young, my mother scolded me. I remember that. And then another time Mother scolded me, and I wanted to commit suicide. My parents never scolded me after that. I myself was surprised later on how I could stand any scolding and harshness from Maharaj—I never felt bad—but even my parents wouldn't dare scold me, because they knew I was very sensitive."

At the age of seven, Swami was sent to school in Vishnupur. "One day in school, the teacher hit me with a cane; and I went to my maternal grandfather, weeping. My grandfather was a lawyer and made the teacher apologize. In fact, he threatened to bring a case against the teacher if he ever hit me again.

"When I was a schoolboy, I had a teacher who used to go to sleep in class. Our classroom had a door to the outside. One day I stealthily went out and brought a goat inside the classroom. The goat began to bleat. The teacher woke up and asked, 'Who did this?' No one would tell him.

"If I felt depressed, my father used to ask me, 'Why are you sad? What would you like?' My parents did not spare anything to please me. Once I told my father, 'I want the works of Girish Ghosh.' He said, 'All right,' and he sent for all of them."

During Swami's early years, he had several encounters with poisonous snakes, which are common in India.

At the time of the first encounter, he was perhaps four years old. One day he and his eight-year-old cousin were jumping off the porch in play. Swami was the younger of the two; he jumped down only a few steps in front of the porch. The older boy jumped straight from the porch down into the garden. After his last jump, the cousin suddenly cried out. Older family members came running and carried the boy inside the house. He had been bitten by a cobra and died.

When Swami was a schoolboy in Vishnupur, he was sitting outdoors one day, studying. It was hot, and he was perspiring. Suddenly he looked up and saw that a small but very poisonous green snake was licking the perspiration on his arm. Swami knew that he should not move suddenly. He kept perfectly still and softly called the cook, "Purna, come! I am in danger!"

The cook heard his call, grabbed a towel, and carefully approached. He quickly threw the towel over Swami's arm and pulled the snake away from him. Swami remembered that he sobbed in relief when the danger was over.

The third snake incident also took place in Vishnupur when Swami was a little older. He had gone into a wooded area to meditate. He was thinking of a forest idyll, such as Rama and Sita had inhabited during their exile. When he stopped meditating, his hand touched the "log" he had been sitting on. Suddenly he realized that he had been sitting on a python. He jumped up and ran home.

By the time Swami had reached his teenage years, Sri Ramakrishna had gone from being "Mad Gadai" to being the most revered living person in Bengal [plate 1]. The small shrine room in the Vishnupur home was called "Thakur's room" ["Master's room," referring to Sri Ramakrishna]. Swami's mother used to do *puja* [ritual worship] there. The worship of Sri Ramakrishna was instituted in the home before Swami joined the monastery. Years later in Vishnupur, a temple to Sri Ramakrishna was built on the ground where Sri Sarada Devi, the Holy Mother, had stood during one of her trips to or from Jayrambati.

The first biography of a holy person that Swami read was that of Sri Chaitanya. He used to reminisce:

"Sri Chaitanya was my first love. When I was thirteen or fourteen years old, I had a private tutor, Rama Akshay Vidyabhusan. He was a very spiritual man. He used to catch us in everything. I saw his yoga powers many times. He asked me to read this book [the *Chaitanya Charitamrita*]. I wept at every page.

"My tutor told me about *The Gospel of Sri Ramakrishna* and introduced me to Swamiji's books and the *Udbodhan* magazine. The tutor was blind. When I read the *Gospel*, the names Rakhal and Naren attracted me.

"In our house in Vishnupur, there were pictures of Thakur, Maharaj [Swami Brahmananda], Swamiji [Swami Vivekananda], and the Hindu Temple of San Francisco, which were given free to subscribers of the *Udbodhan*. The pictures were in the living room. My maternal grandfather used to come and look at them. He would say that their faces looked so soft and tender. In his old age, my grandfather used to read the *Ramakrishna Punthi* and weep.*

"I read *Lectures from Colombo to Almora* [by Swami Vivekananda] in Bengali. I think I was fourteen or fifteen. About the same time I used to read *The Gospel of Sri Ramakrishna* at the Lalbandh"†

Swami Prabhavananda met Holy Mother for the first time in 1907 or 1908.

"One afternoon a friend of mine and I went for a walk in Vishnupur. On the porch of an inn we noticed a swami in *gerua* [ochre] robes surrounded by a number of women, and we thought this not quite proper. But I was curious to find out more about this monk, so after my friend went home, I returned and prostrated before him.

"He inquired, 'Would you like to see Holy Mother?' I had

---

* The *Ramakrishna Punthi* is a life of Ramakrishna in verse form by Akshay Kumar Sen, a lay disciple of Sri Ramakrishna.
† The lake in Vishnupur where Ramakrishna had had the vision of Mrinmayi.

read *The Gospel of Sri Ramakrishna,* so I became quite excited and asked, 'You mean the wife of Ramakrishna Paramahamsa?'

"Holy Mother was sitting within a few feet of me. The swami laughed and said, 'There is Holy Mother. Bow down to her!' I prostrated and touched her feet. And she kissed me as a Bengali mother kisses her grown-up child, touching her fingers to my chin and then to her lips. Then she asked me, 'Child, haven't I seen you before?'

"'No, Mother,' I answered, 'you must have seen my older brother.'

"Much later, when I contemplated this first visit, I felt that I should have answered her differently. I might have said, 'Yes, Mother, you must have known me, because you know all your children. It is we who do not recognize you.'"

Swami Subodhananda was the first monastic disciple of Sri Ramakrishna whom Swami Prabhavananda met. Swami said about their first meeting, "I met him in Vishnupur and took him to my private tutor who was a devotee. He stayed with my tutor."

Within a short time, Swami Prabhavananda accompanied his uncle to Calcutta.

"Amulya, my oldest brother, was studying in Calcutta with Boshi Sen.* They visited Belur Math and took me along. I only knew Swami Subodhananda. That day I met Swami Advaitananda. I prostrated before him. He smiled a little. He looked like a wild man from Borneo. He was unshaven, wore only a loincloth, and was carrying a stick. He was older than Sri Ramakrishna—an old man of eighty. He looked rather wild, and I was frightened."

Around this time Swami Sadananda, Swamiji's first disciple, made a three-month visit to Vishnupur. Boshi Sen introduced Swami Prabhavananda to Swami Sadananda. The Sens were related to Swami Prabhavananda's family and had a home in Vishnupur.

* A plant physiologist who worked under the renowned botanist Jagadish Chandra Bose, who discovered consciousness in plants.

Swami Prabhavananda used to speak of Swami Sadananda's early influence on his life:

"I was fourteen or fifteen years old. I would visit Swami Sadananda after school hours. He told me, 'Abinai [his pet name for Swami], you will go to America to do my Swamiji's work.'

"One day he asked me to bring the dictionary and look up the words *constructive* and *destructive*. Then he repeated three times, 'Be constructive, be constructive, be constructive!'

"Swami Sadananda used to talk to me for hours. Afterward he would say, 'I know you don't understand what I am saying to you now, but I am talking to your subconscious mind. Some day it will all bear fruit.'

"Once Swami Sadananda was eating chicken soup. He fed me some soup with his spoon. I was very orthodox at the time. He broke my orthodoxy.

"Years later, when Swami Sadananda was very ill with diabetes and beriberi, Boshi and Tabu, Boshi's younger brother, were taking care of him. He could not even sit up, and Boshi and his brother thought that he was helpless without them. They did everything for him. Once Swami Sadananda got irritated and said, 'Do you think that I cannot get along without you? Take me and throw me out into the street. You will see—my Swamiji will come and pick me up, and take me on his lap.'"

CHAPTER TWO

The College Years

AT THE AGE of sixteen, Swami Prabhavananda moved to Calcutta in order to attend Calcutta City College. When he first arrived in the city, he was the guest of Boshi Sen. Swami Sadananda was also staying with Boshi at the time. After Swami Prabhavananda's classes started, he moved to a hostel, but he used to visit Swami Sadananda every week.

In the fall of 1910, when Sister Nivedita came to say goodbye to Swami Sadananda before going to Darjeeling for the puja holidays, Swami Prabhavananda's only meeting with Nivedita took place. Swami remembered the scene with amusement: "I wore a gold ring and a gold watch, and had parted my hair. I was known as 'the best-dressed boy in Calcutta.' Nivedita told me that I looked like a sissy and that Swamiji did not like sissies. She asked me who my principal was. I told her. She knew him. I didn't mind what she said. I was fascinated by her voice and intonation."

In 1910 Swami Prabhavananda also met Girish Ghosh, the famous Bengali dramatist and disciple of Sri Ramakrishna whose writings he had requested from his father years before. Swami recalled: "When I met Girish Ghosh, he was saintly. I went to him twice. The first time I went with a swami who was the editor of *Udbodhan*. Ghosh had promised an article or poem for the magazine, and the swami came to ask if it was ready. When we arrived, Girish was dictating a drama. He stopped right then and there and extemporaneously dictated a three-page poem on Sri Ramakrishna.

"The other time I saw Girish, he was once again dictating a drama. I noticed that he would dictate, and then occasionally he would be quiet. He had a bell near him, which he rang occasionally, perhaps to invoke the Presence—I don't know. Then he would dictate again. Why do I say that he was saintly? Because if you sat in his presence in that room, you could feel a holy atmosphere, like in a shrine room."

Swami also saw Girish Ghosh perform in his own dramas. The first performance was in 1910:

"I saw G.C. Ghosh at a benefit performance for the Banaras Home of Service. He took the part of Sadhak in his own play *Vilwamangal*. As he appeared on the stage, someone threw a garland from a box. It fell at his feet. He improvised a line and accepted the garland. His son took the part of Vilwamangal in the play. Tinkori, the famous actress and Girish's protégée, took the part of the Prophetess. This was probably Tinkori's last appearance on the stage. On this benefit night, three plays were given.

"One of the three plays was another of G.C. Ghosh's dramas. It was based on the *Mahabharata*. In this play, Girish Ghosh took the part of a court jester. This jester had the faith that if he chanted the name of God but once, he would be liberated immediately. He went about blindfolded and kept his ears plugged so that he could not see the Lord or hear his name, as he did not want to be liberated yet. Sri Krishna, the divine incarnation, came to town. In spite of the man's precaution, Sri Krishna took away the blindfold, and the man had the vision of Lord Krishna.

"At another time, I saw him in his play *The Life of Shankara*, in which he took the part of an untouchable, a holy man in disguise. And, of course, such was Girish Ghosh himself, a holy man in disguise."

Swami Prabhavananda did not discuss his college studies often. He did mention that for the B.A. degree he studied general philosophy, mathematics, psychology, ethics, and theology—all from the Western perspective.

During his early college life, he became acquainted with Swami Satyakam, a disciple of Holy Mother. Swami Satyakam asked Swami if he wanted to travel to Badri Narayan with him, but when Swami mentioned the invitation to his maternal grandfather, he became upset and would not allow Swami to go.

Although he did not make the pilgrimage to Badri Narayan until he was a *brahmachari* [monastic who has received first vows], Swami went to Puri from Calcutta many times during his student days, sometimes by himself or with two or three friends. He told us: "It was my favorite place of pilgrimage. There are places in Puri where any pilgrim can stay free of charge. For a few pennies you can get *prasad* [sanctified food offered to worshipers] from Jagannath. There is no caste in Puri."

———

Swami Prabhavananda's first meeting with Swami Brahmananda took place in 1911, when Swami was seventeen:

"I learnt that Maharaj had come to Calcutta and was residing at Balaram Babu's house, so I went to visit him there. Maharaj was playing with Mahamaya, Balaram's little granddaughter. Suddenly I felt such an attraction drawing me to Maharaj that I wanted to sit on his lap. Then I left. There was such a large crowd that I knew there was no use trying to see him in Calcutta. I waited for him to go to Belur Math and went to see him there on a weekday.

"Maharaj was seated on the verandah upstairs. It was in the morning, about ten o'clock. He was alone. I did not have the courage to go directly to Maharaj, but I thought to myself, 'Well, I can stand in the corner and watch Swamiji's room; nobody can say anything about that.' But I was really looking at Maharaj. Then he called me, 'Come here.' That was the first thing he said to me. Next he asked, 'Haven't I seen you before? Do you belong to the party of Yogin Thakur [a revolutionary party working for Indian independence]?' I said, 'No, I don't know him.'

"After some talk about where I was studying, and so forth, Maharaj said, 'Could you take these stockings off my feet and put them in the sun?' I remember that it was winter, and he wore maroon-colored socks. I had wanted to touch his feet, and he was giving me that opportunity.

"Then he asked me if I knew how to massage. When I said yes, he allowed me to massage his feet. My feeling at the time was something that I had never felt before in my life: a complete fulfillment in his presence. I cannot express it any other way. You see, he was like a magnet!

"After that I used to go and see him often. I would never talk to him or ask him about religion or spiritual life. I was happy just to be in his company. He would be resting in his room after lunch, and I would slowly open the door and go in and begin to massage his feet.

"Several weeks later an older friend of mine, Sarat Sen, who was my schoolteacher, asked me to introduce him to Maharaj. We both went to see him and were seated at his feet when my friend asked Maharaj for spiritual instructions. I was present while Maharaj told him how to meditate. Afterward Maharaj turned to me and asked, 'Don't you want some instructions?' I said, 'No.'

"On our way home, on the boat, the schoolteacher said, 'He wanted to give you instructions. Why didn't you take any?' 'I don't know,' I replied. 'I felt so shy; I didn't know what to say.'

"I made up my mind to go to Maharaj the next day and ask him for instructions. The schoolteacher accompanied me. As soon as Maharaj saw us, he said, 'Hello, you are here again!'

"'Yes, Maharaj, I want instructions.'

"Maharaj asked the schoolteacher to move away and gave me some preliminary directions on meditation. He told me where to buy rudraksha beads in Calcutta and also asked me to get a little bell to hang around the neck of his pet cow.

"After I brought the beads to Maharaj, he handed them back to me and said, 'Go to the great soul sitting there (he used the word *mahapurusha*) and ask him to show you how to use the beads.'

This was at Belur Math, and the great soul was Swami Atmananda, a disciple of Swamiji. After this, I met Swami Atmananda quite often. He was very devoted to Swamiji."

Maharaj had great affection for Swami Atmananda, who reciprocated with loving reverence for Maharaj. One day, a remarkable conversation took place between them, which Swami Prabhavananda repeated to us:

"Swami Atmananda came by boat from Calcutta. When he got down from the boat, Maharaj saw him and said, 'Sukul Mahashay, accept my *pranam.*' Swami Atmananda immediately replied, 'Maharaj, if you had bowed down to Sukul Mahashay, Sukul Mahashay's head would have separated from the body and fallen at your feet. You have saluted Him who is within me.' And he prostrated before Maharaj."

Swami Prabhavananda never tired of describing the many moods of Maharaj and the effect of his presence on the minds of those who came in contact with him.

"When I met Maharaj, he was living, moving, and having his being in God continuously. The state of *samadhi* [communion with the divine] was natural to him, and he had to struggle at times to bring his mind down to the work of teaching and presiding over the order. The following incident, originally told by Swami Ambikananda, may serve as an illustration:

"A legal document required Maharaj's signature. Three days passed, and Maharaj had not yet signed it. When the secretary came to get the document, he found Maharaj looking at it, pen in hand. An attendant said, 'Please, Maharaj, won't you sign?' Maharaj answered, 'I know, I know; I am trying. But you see, I have forgotten how to write my name.'

"There are certain preliminary signs manifested in a holy man before he plunges into transcendental consciousness. Many times I have witnessed how Maharaj would try to control his samadhi by getting up and walking out of the room. Once I was accusing him of not correcting us (he did plenty of that later). He answered, 'How can I teach all the time? When I see God is playing in every one of you, in so many forms, how can I teach?'

"Maharaj rarely dwelt on spiritual topics. He was religion itself. Just by massaging his feet you received religion.

"Day after day I witnessed a peculiar phenomenon in Maharaj's presence. We disciples would be seated by him in silence. Perhaps we had come to him with problems or worries. No words were spoken, but by the time we left Maharaj's room, our minds were uplifted, and we felt that all our impurities had been washed away. Doubts and disbelief vanished before Maharaj. We did not learn any dogmas or theories about God from him. Maharaj taught us that God *is* and that He can be realized. In his presence, in silence, he would reveal this truth to us.

"Of course, Maharaj was not silent all the time. In one mood he would be playful, like a little boy. He used to tell jokes and funny stories and make us roar with laughter. He taught us that religion is fun. In another state of mind he would be grave and serene; the whole monastery would vibrate with the spiritual atmosphere he created, and we would be afraid to approach, lest we disturb him.

"When spiritual aspirants touched Maharaj's feet, he would relax. When worldly people touched him, he would wince, but this did not mean that he rejected them. It was a purely instinctive reaction. He accepted many such persons, and in so doing he transformed them into devotees."

On those occasions when Maharaj was staying at Belur Math, Swami Prabhavananda used to visit him on weekends. Swami recalled that the hostel staff did not easily give clearance for weekend leave to the students:

"At that time I was studying and living in the hostel of a Brahmo college. Brahmos are somewhat puritanical, and especially on Saturdays and Sundays students were not allowed to go out in the evenings. The theaters were open then, and we were not allowed to attend the theater. Once Maharaj told me, 'Come on a Saturday and stay overnight.' 'But our principal is so strict,' I told him. 'He doesn't permit us to stay out on Saturday nights.' Maharaj then said, 'Ask him anyway; he will give permission.'

"I wrote an application, saying that I would like to visit Belur Math and stay overnight. The superintendent gave his approval. Then I went to the principal, who read the letter and said, 'Take this letter back and write your English correctly.' I read the letter again and again, but I could not find any mistake. Next I took the letter to our English professor. He looked at it and said, 'Put a comma here.' I did so, returned it to the principal, and he granted permission. That is how every weekend I was allowed to go to Belur Math."

Swami Prabhavananda recalled that Maharaj used to take the young devotees fishing with him to give them an opportunity to associate with him:

"I went fishing with Maharaj twice in the Belur Math grounds. It made me nervous. You had to be very careful if he caught a fish to take it off the hook without hurting it and then throw it back in the water.

"A third time I had to hold a hookah for him while he was fishing, and that was hard too.

"Once when he went fishing, there was a big crowd. Ramlal Dada [Sri Ramakrishna's nephew] and Maharaj were both fishing. Maharaj would have us boys throw stones so that Ramlal Dada would not catch any fish."

———

In the fall of 1912, Maharaj went to the Ramakrishna Mission Sevashrama, Kankhal, which is situated on the bank of the Ganges at the foot of the Himalayas. Swami Prabhavananda was particularly fond of relating the episodes that took place during the weeks that followed:

"Although it was during the Durga Puja vacation, which lasted for a month, I was not thinking about the vacation. I was thinking about the money my father had sent to pay my college fees and boarding expenses. I took this money and wrote to my father that I was going to join the monastery, that I still had a number of debts, but would he please ask my brother to come to the hostel to collect my books and other things and settle my affairs. Then I left by train for Hardwar [near Kankhal].

"Banaras was on the way; and as we had to change trains, I visited the Advaita Ashrama.* When the abbot of the ashrama saw me, he said, 'Do you have a letter of introduction?'

"'No,' I told him.

"'Did you write to Maharaj that you are going to Kankhal?'

"'No, he doesn't know I am coming.'

"'Maharaj doesn't like unannounced visitors.'

"I said, 'I have no time to write, and I am going.'

"'But you can't stay here,' he said. 'We don't know you.'† But another swami came to me and said, 'Never mind; don't listen to him. You stay here!' And he went to the abbot and told him, 'I take the responsibility for this young boy; he is no revolutionary.' And so I stayed in Banaras one or two nights.

"When I arrived at the Hardwar station, it was three o'clock in the morning. I hired a horse carriage. It was an hour later and still dark when I entered the monastery grounds in Kankhal. I found myself in the midst of several bungalows, in one of which I might expect to find Maharaj. But in which one? I walked straight to a verandah of one of them, intending to wait beside a door. But before I could sit down, Maharaj himself came out by this same door and Swami Shankarananda, his secretary, by another. I prostrated before Maharaj, and he said simply, 'Hello, you are here.' Then he turned to Swami Shankarananda and told him, 'Make room for this brahmachari. He will be staying.'

"I was then taken to the new building intended for the [tuberculosis] patients, but still unoccupied by them. I was given room in a corner of a large hall. Three other monastics were occupying the other three corners: Swami Madhavananda [then a brahmachari], Brajen, and Dr. Maharaj [Swami Purnananda]. One day Maharaj came to our room and remarked, 'Ah, I see it is crowded here.' Then he added, 'You know, two kings cannot live in one kingdom, but fifty *sadhus* [holy men] can lie under one blanket.'

"Durga Puja was held at the Kankhal sevashrama for the first

* Ramakrishna Advaita Ashrama, Varanasi.
† The Ramakrishna Order swamis were afraid that revolutionaries might implicate the order in political affairs.

time that year, according to Maharaj's wishes. Some devotees brought the image of Mother Durga from Calcutta.

"Lakshman Maharaj, Maharaj's personal attendant, was to be the worshiper for the puja and Swami Shuddhananda, the *tantradharak* [prompter]. Lakshman Maharaj had to learn the ritual, so he had to be released for nearly a month from serving as Maharaj's attendant. Maharaj showed his grace toward me by allowing me to take over Lakshman's duties.

"One day many monks from different orders were invited to partake of the prasad. There was a large crowd of *sannyasis* [wandering mendicants]. I had Maharaj's special chair turned upside down so that nobody else would sit in it. Suddenly I noticed that an elderly swami from another order had set the chair on its feet and was sitting in it. I ran to him and said, 'Sir, you can't sit here.'

"'Why not?'

"'This is our Maharaj's chair, and we don't let anybody else use it.'

"'Oh! But Maharaj won't mind my sitting in his chair!'

"'But I mind!' And I took his hand, intending to pull him up. The swami smiled at me and got up of his own accord.

"Later, as I was placing Maharaj's special asana for him to sit and partake of the prasad, he noticed this and told me, 'Oh, no! No special seat for me. There are several great souls here today.'

"When the swamis gathered on the verandah, four elderly monks who did not belong to our order were seated on either side of Maharaj. And the swami I had pulled out of the chair was in the place of honor, to Maharaj's right. They were talking and laughing—and I had the distinct impression that they were having a good laugh at my expense. However, Maharaj never mentioned the matter to me.

"One day at Kankhal, I was meditating alone when the abbot of a well-known Shankara order entered the room. He was dressed in silk robes and wore a jeweled turban. Seeing me seated in meditation, he said, 'Ah, he is in samadhi!' When I heard this, I burst out laughing, got up, and bowed to him."

Swami Prabhavananda used to say that it is a great blessing to have the *darshan* [experience] of guru and Ganges together at the same time. In this connection he would recall the immersion of Mother Durga's image in Kankhal in 1912:

"Maharaj and all the swamis and brahmacharis went to the bank of the Ganges. Two boats had been hired. The image was placed in one of the boats, accompanied by the swamis. Both boats left for the immersion, which was to be near some special landing ghat. Maharaj did not go. He was still standing on the bank of the Ganges, and I was standing near him. He said, 'You did not go!' 'No, Maharaj.'

"It was the hour of sunset. As was his custom at that hour, Maharaj folded his palms and saluted the Lord for a few minutes. He asked me to sprinkle some Ganges water on him, which I did. Then, while he was saluting the Lord and standing on the bank of the Ganges, I prostrated at his feet. This sacred moment stands out vividly in my memory.

"After the immersion of the image, Vijaya was observed. We all sat together in rows. I was behind Maharaj and Swami Turiyananda. Maharaj asked us all to chant 'Jaya Sri Durga.' Then each one was served *siddhi*, a mind-altering drink, in a small earthen cup. Once a year, during Vijaya, it is the custom to take a sip of siddhi as a sacrament. Siddhi can produce psychedelic effects, but only when taken in large amounts. Maharaj touched his lips to the drink and saw me seated behind him. He offered me the cup, and I drank. Swami Turiyananda touched the drink with his lips the same way and then, turning back, offered me the cup. I drank again. This was the first time in my life that I had ever drunk siddhi. Later, as Swami Turiyananda was seated on the verandah in a chair and some of us were standing before him, listening to him, I was suddenly seized with a fit of laughter. Swami Turiyananda looked at my eyes and said, 'Abani, go to bed.' I went to bed and slept soundly. The drink did not have any bad effect on me.

"I was very fond of Bengali sweetmeats, which were unavailable at Kankhal. One day Maharaj said to me, 'Abani, you must be missing the sweets of Bengal. But you know, if you make japa and wish for anything, it will come to you.' He closed his eyes for a minute, counted on his fingers and made japa. Within an hour, three Bengali women arrived from Meerut with rasagollas and sandesh for Maharaj—my favorite sweets. These were offered to the Lord, and we all partook of the prasad. I thought that Maharaj had received news in advance that the Bengali devotees were coming that morning and that he had played a joke on me. I approached the devotees and asked them, 'Mothers, did you write to Maharaj that you were coming here this morning?' They replied, 'No, we wanted to surprise Maharaj, so we didn't let him know that we were coming.' I asked them, 'But do you bring sweets every time you come to visit Maharaj?' They answered, 'Oh, no, this is the first time we have brought sweets.' Then I realized that my guess was wrong.

"A boy of my age, who was the son of a disciple of Maharaj, came to Kankhal. After the Durga Puja, this boy and I went to visit Hrishikesh and Swargashram. We went by horse carriage to Hrishikesh and from there crossed the bridge over the Ganges and went to Swargashram. It was at that time a very lonely place, with a few cottages scattered here and there for the sadhus to live and practice meditation. In one cottage, we found a young sadhu suffering from fever. I left what money I had in the cottage, hoping it might help him in some way. We returned to Hrishikesh. Both of us were hungry. I had spent all the money I had brought with me, expecting that the other boy had some money with him. But he had none. Both of us sat in an inn, not knowing what to do or how to go back to Kankhal. We could not walk back and were beginning to get worried. Just then some devotees of the math [monastery] arrived. They quickly prepared food and invited us to partake of it. And they had room in their horse carriage for us, so that we got back safely to Kankhal.

"When Maharaj saw me, he exclaimed, 'Why, you look so tired and thin!' Mahapurush Maharaj [Swami Shivananda] was there. He remarked, 'He must have practiced some austerity at Hrishikesh.' Maharaj said, 'Austerity! Nonsense! He had to undergo some hardship for some reason.' I remained silent. Later, when I was alone, I wept, thinking of Maharaj's affection for me.

"I used to light a charcoal fire for Maharaj's hubble-bubble. He would take a few puffs and become absorbed. Suddenly he would say, 'Hey, there is no fire.' I would relight it. Again he would become absorbed. During that time he used to converse with gods and goddesses. No one else saw anything, and there was no outward change in Maharaj, except that his eyes had that indrawn look.

"Maharaj had a servant whose name was Bulbul. I was jealous of him. He was doing so many things for Maharaj that I could not do. And I learnt my lesson trying to do them. Once Maharaj asked me to tell Bulbul to heat water for his bath. I did not tell him. I myself built the fire and heated the water. Then Maharaj asked me, 'What pot did you use to heat the water?' I told him. He said, 'You didn't know that I have a special pot.' Then I had to take recourse to Bulbul after all to get the other pot and heat the water. I learnt my lesson.

"I stayed in Kankhal for a month and then was initiated. When I expressed my desire to join the monastery, Maharaj asked me to go back to college and finish my education. I told him that my father might force me to get married. Then Maharaj said, 'In that case, run away and come to me.' Two years later, I joined the order, which Maharaj knew was to be my destiny, as he had called me 'brahmachari' when I first arrived in Kankhal."

Before Swami Prabhavananda left Kankhal to return to Calcutta, Maharaj asked him to visit Allahabad and Vrindaban. It was during this pilgrimage to Vrindaban, in 1912, that Swami Prabhavananda's meeting with a holy man took place, which he often referred to in later years:

"I asked if there was a Vaishnava sadhu living in Vrindaban whom I might see. I was told that Swami Turiyananda used to visit a certain one, known to be living in a forest nearby. So I followed a narrow path, which led to a clearing with a small hut in the center. Soon the sadhu came out of the hut. His disciple spread a mat for him on the ground. He sat on the mat and motioned to me to be seated too. There was an uplifting atmosphere in the presence of this holy man. I bowed down to him and asked, 'Revered sir, how did you attain this state?' He answered my question in just one word: '*Nama*,' the name of the Lord. I stayed for a little while in silence, and then saluted him and came away."

During his college years, Swami Prabhavananda became interested in India's independence movement. His involvement in anti-British activities appears to have peaked between the fall of 1912 (after Maharaj had asked him to finish his college education) and the winter of 1914. Swami explained, "I didn't lose interest in Maharaj or in religion. But I thought to free India is Swamiji's work. I decided that I would remain unmarried and devote my life to the freedom of India. But I always kept in touch with Maharaj."

Swami contributed to the cause of independence by writing leaflets urging young men to revolt against British rule.

On one occasion he invited Rashbehari Bose, the famous Indian revolutionary, to his father's home. Bose had thrown a bomb at Lord Hardinge [Viceroy of India]. Swami's older brother recognized Rashbehari after seeing his picture in a newspaper, and he wanted to show the paper to their father. But Swami took the paper away and burnt it. Rashbehari left, and Kumud Ghosh never learned the identity of his guest.

Swami's principal at the college, Mr. Maitra, once protected Swami from the police by advising him to get rid of any incriminating evidence he might have in his possession. The warning was timely, as Swami was then hiding in his room at the hostel several revolvers for the revolutionaries.

Once, in 1914, a revolutionary activist came to Swami's room at three o'clock in the morning to wake him up. Swami looked out of the window and saw six or seven bullock carts, covered with tarpaulins, lined up in the street. Swami was told that under the tarpaulins were stolen rifles and ammunition; but now that they had them, the revolutionaries did not know where to take them. Swami recommended that they pile the equipment in a boat and take it to an acquaintance of his in Chandannagor, the French possession, where the British could not confiscate it. Swami supplied the address of his acquaintance in Chandannagor. Later that morning, the newspapers were full of the theft. The equipment was never traced.

In 1914 Swami Prabhavananda received his B.A. degree from Calcutta City College and proceeded to study for six months at Calcutta University toward an M.A. degree. As Swami related:

"For the M.A., I took philosophy and nothing else. Our professor was Brajendra Nath Seal. He was senior to Swami Vivekananda in the same college. They used to debate with each other. Professor Seal contributed some writing for Swamiji's biography.

"Before admitting us to his class, Professor Seal sent for each of us to come to his room privately. First, he asked us if we knew Sanskrit well. The most difficult Sanskrit is Ramanuja's; Shankara's Sanskrit is easy. But he tested us with Ramanuja's Sanskrit. When it was my turn, he asked me to read and then explain. I did, and so I was admitted into the class. I was twenty years old—the youngest in the class.

"One day [some months later] Professor Seal noticed that I had not been attending class for a few weeks. He asked, 'Where is that boy?' A friend who knew me well explained that I had joined the Belur Math. The professor was quiet for a moment. Then he asked, 'Do the authorities of the Belur Math forbid him to come to my class because the class is open to the public?' Then my friend told him, 'No, it is not that. But he is not in Calcutta, and it would be difficult to come.'

"Professor Seal was a fine speaker. It was wonderful to listen to him. He took the last hour of the day so that he could lecture for two hours.

"Later, when I was a brahmachari in Madras, Professor Seal became the vice-chancellor of Mysore University. He wrote a letter to our monastery in Madras requesting accommodation for a few hours. I went to receive him at the station. Of course, he did not recognize me."

During his college years, Swami Prabhavananda used to spend a month at a time with Maharaj during the summers and puja vacations. Although before he joined the monastery his association was primarily with Maharaj, he also was blessed with opportunities to receive the darshan of Holy Mother. Swami used to go to the Udbodhan Office in Calcutta on Saturdays, when men were permitted to prostrate before Holy Mother, as he often related in later years:

"People would line up for blocks just to bow down to her. Every time I went and touched Holy Mother's feet, I invariably had the same peculiar experience. In a way, it can be compared to that of receiving an electric shock. Of course, when one touches a live wire, one recoils in pain. But what she communicated by her touch was a very pleasant sensation, which made me feel purified, though I did not at that time realize its full significance.

"I had been told that one could talk freely with Holy Mother if one went to see her in her village. She wore a veil in Calcutta and went without a veil only in Jayrambati. So, after my initiation by Maharaj, I went to Jayrambati with a friend of mine, who also later became a swami. Being young and thoughtless, we had not remembered to let Holy Mother know in advance about our visit. But it turned out to be unnecessary. When we arrived, her attendant informed us that she was expecting us and that she had told him to make room for two of 'Rakhal's [Maharaj's] children' who were coming.

"We reached Jayrambati after the noonday meal was finished, but Holy Mother had kept aside some food for us. Our lunch was served on leaf plates, and she sat by us and we talked. Afterward we got up to remove our plates, but Holy Mother said, 'What are you doing?' My friend was shy in her presence, but I answered boldly, 'Mother, we must not leave these plates here!' She replied, 'What would you do in your own home if your mother were sitting beside you?' That settled it; she cleaned up after us.

"There was an extraordinary quality about Holy Mother. She seemed to many who met her exactly like their own mother. I had this impression, and I have asked others who confirmed it. Unaware as I was then of her spiritual greatness, I thought of Holy Mother as an ordinary country woman—simple and natural, just like my own mother. But something happened within me then, which I did not realize until much later. Now I would say that I received the grace of Maharaj and of the Ramakrishna Order because I received Mother's grace first."

Swami Prabhavananda also had the blessing of associating with some of Sri Ramakrishna's monastic disciples besides Maharaj, in Calcutta as well as at the various maths of the Ramakrishna Order. Swami Subodhananda, whom Swami had already met in Vishnupur, occasionally visited him in Calcutta. Swami Subodhananda was known as "Khoka Maharaj," literally "Baby Maharaj," because he was so young when he first came to Sri Ramakrishna. Swami Prabhavananda used to comment on Khoka Maharaj's unassuming ways:

"He was just like a friend. He would send a note to our college for me through our gatekeeper. I used to make a chocolate drink. He would come to our hostel sometimes and share it. I was between seventeen and nineteen years old then."

In October 1914, Swami Prabhavananda visited Banaras. Swamis Brahmananda, Premananda, and Turiyananda were then staying at the Ramakrishna Advaita Ashrama and Mission Home of Service, and Swami Prabhavananda recalled his intimate association with them:

"In Banaras, Maharaj used to ask Swami Premananda to take me with him to the Ganges for a bath and then to the Vishwanath and Annapurna temples. We went every day for a month. In the crowd, Swami Premananda would hold my hand and draw me after him. When he did that, what a thrill I got!

"First we would bathe in the Ganges. Then he would change his cloth. I would wash his wet cloth and carry it, and carry his towel and vessel of Ganges water. I used to follow Swami Premananda and would take the mud from his footprints and put it on my body. I had such reverence for him! After we came home, he would wash his feet, and I would dry them. Those were the days! To walk with gods!

"Before Swami Premananda entered the Vishwanath Temple, he would buy some flowers. Then we would enter the temple. After he bathed Lord Shiva [the linga], he would give me the waterpot, and I would pour water to bathe Lord Shiva. Afterward, as is the custom, we used to circumambulate the shrine. Near the shrine there is a little bench made of cement. He would ask me to sit beside him on the bench and make japa.

"Next we used to go to the temple of the Divine Mother, Annapurna. One day, as we were finishing the worship of Mother Annapurna, the head priest of the temple, who knew Swami Premananda, placed a garland of marigolds around the swami's neck. Swami Premananda's color was beautiful. I have never seen any Hindu with such beautiful golden skin! When he wanted to take the garland off to give it to me, I said to him with folded palms, 'No Maharaj, please keep the garland yourself. You look so beautiful!' The word *beautiful* reminded Swami Premananda of God's beauty, and he went into ecstasy. His face flushed, and his mind became completely indrawn. A light emanated from his whole body. It was just like an electric bulb lighting up.

"Walking slowly, Swami Premananda left the temple, and I followed him. The temple lane of Vishwanath was crowded as usual, but on both sides of us people stared at him and made way. It was evident that everyone present saw his transfiguration. We continued to walk through the streets of Banaras while crowds stood still, silently watching Swami Premananda. His eyes were cast down; he was absorbed in the thought of God and completely oblivious of his surroundings. It was about a mile from the temple to the monastery. When we came to the ashrama gate, Swami Nirbharananda, the abbot, saw us from the verandah. He called out, 'Boys, prepare a royal welcome for Swami Premananda!' We entered the monastery grounds to the sound of gongs, bells, and conch shells. When we arrived at the verandah of the ashrama, Swami Premananda took the garland off and placed it on Swami Nirbharananda. Then he danced, still in ecstasy. Slowly his mind regained external consciousness, and the divine light disappeared.

"One day I was present when Swami Premananda said to Maharaj, 'Let us get rid of this gerua cloth. It advertises that we are monks.' He was in such a mood of renunciation that even the traditional monastic dress seemed to him a barrier before complete self-effacement."

Swami Prabhavananda had the opportunity to observe Maharaj and his brother disciples in many different moods. Maharaj had a keen sense of humor. With the help of the young devotees, he sometimes played practical jokes on some of his brothers, Swami Premananda being a favorite target. Swami Prabhavananda recalled participating on two such occasions:

"Maharaj used to tease Swami Premananda through me in an affectionate way. Once, while I was massaging Maharaj, he whispered to me, 'Go to Brother Baburam in the next room and give him a massage.' Now, Swami Premananda was not in the habit of accepting personal service from anyone and never let himself be massaged. But as Maharaj had given me this order, I meant to carry it out. I went to Swami Premananda's room and opened the door. The swami was lying on his cot, covered with a sheet. I took one of his feet and began to massage. Swami Premananda sat up and said, 'Go away! I don't want a massage. Go to Maharaj!' But I did not listen to his protests. Again I pulled his leg toward me and began to massage, explaining, 'Maharaj asked me to do it.' This continued for some time. Every time the swami objected, I told him I had to carry out Maharaj's order. Finally he relaxed, and I gave him a good massage. I was blessed to serve him.

"When I came to Banaras, I had brought with me two bottles of Welch's grape juice for Maharaj. As soon as Maharaj saw the bottles of grape juice, he said, 'Get a glass.' I got a glass. He poured the juice and said, 'Take this glass to Swami Premananda in the Advaita Ashrama and tell him that this is the finest wine you could find in Calcutta." So I went, placed the glass before Swami Premananda, and told him what Maharaj had instructed me to say. Swami Premananda said, 'Take it away! Get away from here!' But I would not leave him alone. Swami Premananda got up from his chair and went to the end of the wall in the garden while I followed him with the glass. Then Maharaj arrived. (He always walked very softly, and we often did not know when he had arrived on the scene.) Maharaj said, 'Baburam-da, why don't you drink that? It's only some grape juice he has brought for you.' Then Swami Premananda said, 'Why didn't the rascal tell me!'"

In whatever monastery Maharaj was staying, he was keenly observant of the details of service and particularly so pertaining to the ritual worship in the temples. Swami Prabhavananda remembered the following incident: "One morning when I was gathering tulsi [a kind of sacred basil] leaves, Maharaj asked me, 'Why are you gathering tulsi leaves?' I replied, 'Baburam Maharaj has asked me.' Baburam Maharaj was present. Maharaj asked him, 'Baburam-da, I hope you are not going to worship Lord Shiva with tulsi leaves!'* Swami Premananda answered, 'Oh no, not for worshiping Lord Shiva, but for the worship of Mother Ganges.' Then Maharaj said, 'That's all right.'

"I have seen Swami Premananda prostrate full length [*sashtanga* pranam] before Maharaj. Swami Premananda once said to Maharaj, 'You are the presiding deity in all our sacrifices—our Yajneshwar Hari.'

"Swami Premananda wanted Maharaj to come to the Belur Math. But Maharaj didn't want to leave Banaras. He said, 'This is Shiva's place.' Swami Premananda argued, 'But Belur Math is also Shiva's place.' Finally Swami Premananda prostrated before Maharaj and said, 'Unless you give your word that you will come to Belur Math, I will not get up.' Maharaj's face became very serious, and he said, 'All right, Baburam-da, I will come.'"

While Swami Prabhavananda was in Banaras, *Karma Yoga* was read at the monastery. Swami related: "Swami Premananda, who

---

* Shiva is traditionally worshiped with bel leaves, never with tulsi leaves.

attended regularly, remarked one day, 'Ah, this *Karma Yoga* of Swamiji is *jnana* yoga.'"*

During his stay in Banaras in 1914, Swami Prabhavananda also studied the Brahma Sutras with Shankara's commentary under Swami Turiyananda. "I would argue with Swami Turiyananda about Brahman and *maya* [illusion]," Swami Prabhavananda reminisced. "I was full of Western philosophy at that time. During the classes, I used to quote Western philosophers, and I would argue from their point of view. But we never argued with Maharaj. The other young disciples sometimes thought I was impertinent, but I knew Swami Turiyananda liked our discussions and encouraged me.

"Later, when I was in Calcutta, Swami Achalananda wrote, requesting me to send some green coconuts for Swami Turiyananda. On receiving the coconuts, Swami Achalananda wrote, saying that Swami Turiyananda had asked him to write: 'The classes have become insipid and dull. There is not much discussion.' Also, he said that Swami Turiyananda missed me."

Once, possibly in Banaras, Swami asked Swami Turiyananda to teach him how to study the Gita. Swami Turiyananda advised him to take one verse at a time, meditate on its meaning, and live the verse for a week before going on to the next verse. In that way he was to study the entire Gita.

In later years, Swami Prabhavananda related the following incidents that took place in Banaras and also concerned several direct disciples of Sri Ramakrishna:

"One day in Banaras, Maharaj and Swami Turiyananda were seated on the cemented circle around the bel tree, meditating. Swami Atmananda was seated below them, meditating too. A woman devotee came and bowed before Maharaj and Swami Turiyananda. She was known as a great devotee. Her name was Maji. Swami Atmananda got up to leave. Maharaj asked him, 'Why are you leaving?' Swami Atmananda replied, 'Well, I am

---

* Cf. Bhagavad Gita 5.4: "The yoga of action, say the ignorant, is different from the yoga of the knowledge of Brahman. The wise see knowledge and action as one: they see truly."

a monk.' Maharaj asked him, 'Then what are we?' Swami Atmananda answered, 'You are *paramahamsas* [spiritual teachers
who have attained enlightenment]!'

"Another day a swami, in the presence of Swami Premananda and many others, began to argue with me, saying that Swamiji was a qualified monist and not a nondualist. I argued back
that this wasn't true. And then we raised our voices. It caused a
sensation and ended on a rather sorry note. Swami Achalananda was then Swami Turiyananda's attendant and reported
the discussion to Swami Turiyananda. Of course I was feeling
very bad. Swami Turiyananda sent for me. He told me, 'Don't
you remember what Shankara said? There are two kinds of argument: one is to discuss in order to arrive at the truth. This is
called real argument. The other is to forcibly establish one's
opinion. This is not called argument.'"

Swami Prabhavananda also mentioned an episode concerning Maharaj and Swami Shivananda. Mahapurush Maharaj had
been staying in Almora and was to come to Banaras.

"Maharaj made arrangements to greet Swami Shivananda
with honor and respect. Swami Shivananda missed the train
and arrived in Banaras several hours later than expected. When
Mahapurush Maharaj was told about the reception Maharaj
had planned for him, he said, 'It is right that I couldn't come. I
couldn't have accepted such honor and respect from Maharaj.'"

During his Christmas vacation of 1914, Swami Prabhavananda
visited Belur Math. Maharaj had returned to Belur Math from
Banaras. At this time, Swami Prabhavananda was studying the
Brahma Sutras with Shankara's commentary under Swami
Shuddhananda, a disciple of Swamiji. Swami Prabhavananda
related:

"As we studied, Swami Shuddhananda would argue with me,
wanting me to join the monastery. And I would argue back that
the monks were lazy people because they were not doing Swamiji's work. We student revolutionaries were the ones who followed Swamiji, because Swamiji wanted India to be free. Swami

Shuddhananda could not convince me otherwise. There was an old man who used to listen to all of this. Every morning it was customary for us to go and prostrate before Maharaj. One day this old man followed me when I went to prostrate, and he said to Maharaj, 'Maharaj, when is this boy going to be a monk?'

"Maharaj kept silent for a moment. Then, looking at me from head to foot, he said, 'When the Lord wills.' As he looked at me, there was an unforgettable sweetness in his eyes, and a sudden transformation took place within me. My whole idea of revolution and all it entailed changed in an instant. I did not say anything to Maharaj but went downstairs and told Swami Shuddhananda, 'I have joined the monastery.'"

Plate 1. Ramakrishna at Dakshineswar

Plate 2. Sarada Devi, the Holy Mother, Udbodhan, 1909

CHAPTER THREE

From Belur Math to Puri

SWAMI PRABHAVANANDA AND his friend Paresh, who later became Swami Amriteshwarananda, joined the Belur monastery on the same day in December 1914. About a month later, on Swami Vivekananda's birthday, they were to receive their first monastic vows along with about two dozen other probationers. Swami Prabhavananda related, "Maharaj wanted all those who were to be given *brahmacharya* [first monastic vows] to be recommended by Swami Premananda. One day Paresh and I were seated at Maharaj's feet. He looked at us and said, 'You two don't need any recommendation.'

"The day of brahmacharya, Khoka Maharaj said to me, 'Take a cup of tea. It will be all right.' It is usual to observe a complete fast on the day of taking monastic vows, but he poured a cup of tea for me. Before I got it to my lips, Maharaj came downstairs and said, 'What are you doing?' I explained, 'Khoka Maharaj said it would be all right for me to have a cup of tea.'

"Maharaj said, 'No!' I put the cup down.

"About one or two o'clock in the afternoon, I was giving Maharaj a massage. He said to me, 'You look so bad. Take some fruit!' I replied, 'I can manage all right without it.' But Maharaj told me, 'No, go and take some fruit prasad.'"

Maharaj initiated Swami into brahmacharya and gave him the name Bhakti Chaitanya.

Swami's parents were quite upset by this turn of events and wanted him to come to Vishnupur for a visit. "After many entreaties I had to agree," Swami recalled. "Maharaj was then staying at Balaram Bose's house in Calcutta.* I went there and told him of my parents' wish. He said, 'Yes, go!' Before I took leave of Maharaj, he introduced me to Ramakrishna Babu, Balaram's son. As he did so, he rubbed my shaven head. He bestowed something with that touch. I did not say when I would return to the math. It turned out that I was delayed for a month."

Swami's father was very attached to his son Abani and wept when Swami wanted to return to Belur Math. His mother, too, wanted him to stay on in Vishnupur. One night Swami borrowed money from a friend and went to the railway station without informing his family. In the meantime his mother had discovered that Swami's belongings were missing, so she sent Swami's oldest brother, Amulya, to bring him back. "It was two o'clock in the morning," Swami remembered. "I had bought my ticket and was about to get into the train when Amulya arrived at the station and said, 'Mother is weeping. You should have told her you were leaving. Come back and stay three or four more days. Then she will let you go.' And that is what happened. Within a week my parents gave me the money to leave."

During the month Swami Prabhavananda spent at Vishnupur, he did not write to anyone at the math about returning. One morning at the Belur monastery, Maharaj asked Paresh, "When is Abani coming back?"

Paresh replied sadly, "Oh, Maharaj, I haven't heard from him at all. I don't think he is coming back."

But Maharaj said, "He is coming back this morning." An hour later Swami Prabhavananda walked through the door.

His friend Paresh afterward told him that Maharaj had known about his coming, although Swami had not written.

Shortly after Swami Prabhavananda joined the monastery, his favorite niece died. In Swami's words:

* Balaram Bose was a a lay disciple of Sri Ramakrishna.

"My brother Amulya's daughter Suprabha was very attached to me; and I, to her. She was six or seven years old. One day she told my sister, 'Don't tell Grandma, but I won't go to school today. They are coming here in a chariot to get me. Don't tell Grandma; she won't let me go.' When my mother realized that Suprabha hadn't gone to school, she asked her, 'What is the matter?' Suprabha answered, 'Grandma, I don't feel good.' My mother felt her forehead. She had a high fever. A few hours later she was gone. Before she died, she asked for a picture of me. Holding the picture tightly, she passed away."

———————

Swami Prabhavananda's first months at Belur Math were spent in close association with several direct disciples of Sri Rama-krishna, particularly Maharaj and Swamis Premananda and Subodhananda. Swami Prabhavananda used to tell us about those unforgettable days.

"Swami Premananda taught me one of my first lessons on the behavior of a saint. Just after I had joined, I happened to be present while he scolded another boy vehemently. I thought to myself, 'Ah, this holy man loses his temper.' As soon as this thought crossed my mind, Swami Premananda looked at me and smiled. He immediately gave me to understand that he was not really angry, but that he was making a show of anger in order to teach the boy a lesson.

"When I first joined the monastery, Swami Premananda would take me with him to various places. But he never just asked me to accompany him. He always went to see Maharaj first. Then he would say to me, 'Maharaj wants you to go with me.' Once Swami Premananda took me with him when he was to preside at a meeting at Salkia, a village near the monastery where the devotees were celebrating the birthday anniversary of Swamiji. I was a brahmachari then. Swami Premananda had me sit with him on the speaker's platform. There were several speakers present besides Swami Premananda. While Swami was introducing them, I had a premonition that he would ask me to speak too. I prayed fervently that he would change his mind. While returning with Swami in the carriage, he told me that he was about to ask me to say something but decided against doing so. Then I said to him, 'Yes, Maharaj, I know; and I was praying fervently that you would not. The Lord listened to my prayer.' He simply smiled.

"After Swami Trigunatita had died, the devotees in San Francisco wanted another direct disciple of Thakur to come. They wanted Swami Premananda. Harihar (later Vasudevananda) and I were then brahmacharis at Belur Math. One day Swami Premananda said to us, 'Boys, read the Bible and get ready to come with me to America!' We knew, of course, that it was only a pipe dream, but we read the Bible. Then Maharaj dampened the spirit."

Recalling those early days spent in Maharaj's holy company, Swami Prabhavananda mentioned to us that he saw Maharaj hold a book in his hands only twice. "The first time was when he asked me to pick out some chants to learn. The other time was when he had decided to send me to Mayavati in the Himalayas. That time he gave me a philosophical treatise on the nondual aspect of Vedanta and asked me to read it to him. Of course, this was for my benefit. Maharaj did not need to read books or scriptures. He was a *brahmarshi*, a knower of Brahman. I remember that my voice was changing at that time. While I was reading, my voice broke, and I was very embarrassed."

"Shortly after I had joined the monastery, I followed Maharaj around for a whole day. Finally he went to his room. He lay down, and I massaged his feet. I said, 'Please, Maharaj, give me samadhi!'

"Maharaj kept silent. I persisted, 'Maharaj, please give me that touch!' Then he said, 'Ah, you are so impatient!'

"Another day, later, I was coming out of Maharaj's room when he followed me and stopped me. He said, 'Look, what is to happen to you after death I have done for you. But, my child, if you wish to enjoy the bliss of God in this life, you must struggle for it.'"

Maharaj showed his grace in different ways, suiting the needs and circumstances of particular devotees, as related by Swami Prabhavananda in the two following incidents:

"An eighteen-year-old student, studying in the Metropolitan College in Calcutta, was reading in the library [probably at Belur Math]. Maharaj entered the room and asked the boy to hold his hand. The boy went into samadhi. Maharaj locked the door. After a couple of hours Maharaj opened the door and brought him out of that state. No one knows what happened to the boy later."

The second incident concerns Boshi Sen's younger brother. "Tabu was loved by Holy Mother, Maharaj, and all the swamis. Once he did something he felt he should not have done and afterward avoided Maharaj. He would visit the younger swamis and then slip away. One day Maharaj caught him and said, 'Tabu, do you know that buffaloes have big horns where flies can sit and the buffaloes don't feel anything?' Maharaj opened his arms wide and added, 'I have big horns like that.'"

During this period at Belur Math, Swami Prabhavananda shared a room with Swamis Subodhananda, Ambikananda, and Shankarananda. As the most junior of the four, he was sometimes required to move, depending on the number of guests visiting the monastery. In later years, Swami often recalled Swami Subodhananda's affectionate concern for him on one of these occasions.

"Swami Premananda would invite guests, so I had to give up my bed. One day Baburam Maharaj brought a guest and told me to go somewhere else. Khoka Maharaj said, 'Abani, come and sleep in my bed.' And, of course, I did. But I couldn't sleep all night, worrying whether my feet might touch him.

"Whenever Maharaj sat on anyone's bed in that room, he sat on Khoka Maharaj's bed."

Swami heard the following reminiscences directly from Khoka Maharaj:

"When Khoka Maharaj first came to Sri Ramakrishna, he was a boy of fourteen or fifteen. Thakur asked him, 'Aren't you the grandson of Shankar Ghosh?' Khoka Maharaj answered him, 'Yes, but how do you know?' Thakur replied, 'Oh, I knew thirty years ago that you were to be born there [in that family].'

"Thakur had long hair. Khoka Maharaj parted Thakur's hair and put a mirror in front of him. Thakur smiled and said, 'Oh, you are making me a *babu* [a dandy].'

"Once Thakur caught a little cold, and Khoka Maharaj suggested, 'Take a cup of tea, and you will be cured.' Thakur smiled.

"After Sri Ramakrishna's passing away, Khoka Maharaj practiced austerities in the Himalayas. In Hrishikesh he once fell ill with a high fever. He had a vision of Thakur, who asked him, 'Shall I send you a rich Marwari [a member of an Indian ethnic group] to take care of you?' Khoka Maharaj answered, 'No, I would rather be ill and have you sit by me.' Then Thakur touched him, and he got well.

"One day Swamiji asked Khoka Maharaj to speak. Khoka Maharaj dressed like Swamiji with a turban. Just as he was about to speak there was an earthquake, and everyone left. Swamiji said, 'When Khoka got up to speak, he shook the earth.'

"Khoka Maharaj once told us about an experience he had, but he told it in the third person so that nobody would know who it was:

"A devotee went on a pilgrimage to Kedarnath. This temple is located very high in the Himalayas; therefore it is closed half the year during the snow season. The devotee arrived just as the last priests were leaving, before the heavy snows came. He and one priest were the only ones there. He went into the temple and made his offering to the Lord. Then the snow began coming down. It was so heavy that the devotee couldn't leave the temple, so the priest suggested that they play a game of chess. They played all night, and the next morning the snow stopped. The devotee could go on his way home. He didn't realize that six months had passed. Khoka Maharaj said to us, 'It was Lord Shiva who came in the form of the priest.' The way Khoka Maharaj told the story, I knew that he himself was the devotee who had played chess with Lord Shiva.

"Once Swamiji, Maharaj, and Khoka Maharaj shared the same room. Swamiji was meditating; the others were asleep. After a while Swamiji asked, 'Khoka, are you awake? Can you prepare a chillum of tobacco for me?' When Khoka Maharaj had done it, Swamiji was so satisfied that he told him, 'Ask a boon of me.'

"'Why should I accept a boon from you? I have got everything from Thakur.'

"Maharaj remarked, 'Khoka, Swamiji is in a mood. Ask for something.'

"Then Khoka Maharaj said, 'All right, give me this boon— that wherever I may be, I may have a cup of tea at least once a day.' Swamiji said, 'Granted.'"

Swami Prabhavananda added, "Once I asked Khoka Maharaj, 'Have you always had your cup of tea?' He answered, 'Yes, every day, at least before I went to bed at night, I had a cup of tea. Once it happened in a very strange way. As I was walking in the Himalayas, at eight or nine in the evening, I saw some Marwari gentlemen seated. They invited me for a cup of tea.'"

Swami heard the following story from another monk. "Khoka Maharaj had many visions. Yet one day he said, 'I don't trust visions.' Those who were present were amazed. Then Khoka Maharaj added, 'But now I have reached the state where I know that the Atman [the Spirit, or Self] is separate from the body.'"

————

It was in 1915, not long after Swami Prabhavananda had received the vows of brahmacharya, that Maharaj decided to send him to the Advaita Ashrama in Mayavati. Swami recalled, "When Maharaj was about to send me to Mayavati, he gave a big lecture against life at Belur Math, saying, 'Here devotees take you in motor cars. That is not spiritual life.'"

Before Swami left for Mayavati, Maharaj said to him, "Keep your mind as high as the Himalayas." This much has been previously published, but Swami Prabhavananda did not divulge the full details of Maharaj's parting advice until five months before his own death. In February 1976, Swami related the incident completely:

"When Maharaj sent me to Mayavati, he said, 'Just as Sri Krishna sent Uddhava to Badri Narayan to practice meditation, so am I sending you to Mayavati in the Himalayas. Keep your mind tuned as high as the Himalayas.'" Then Swami added, "You can say this after my death."

On another occasion, Swami Prabhavananda continued his memories of that period in his life. "Before I went to Mayavati, Maharaj asked me to get Holy Mother's blessings. Three of us went. Holy Mother gave each of us a flower and kissed us." Swami explained that Holy Mother had touched her fingers to each one's chin and then to her lips. Swami told this story only seven weeks before he passed away. He added, "The picture you see in my room is the way I saw her then. She took the Devi *murti* [form of the Divine Mother]. She appeared very tall." The picture of Holy Mother to which Swami referred was the one he asked to have framed and hung in his room in Hollywood during the last three months of his life [plate 2].

Swami Prabhavananda was particularly fond of recalling the following incidents from his early days as a brahmachari:

"When I was twenty-two years old, I stopped in Varanasi on my way to Mayavati in the Himalayas. There I fell ill with chicken pox mixed with smallpox. Hari Maharaj [Swami Turiyananda] would not let me proceed further. Swami Atmabodhananda had already had the disease, so he took care of me. I had a high fever.

"Every day Swami Turiyananda would come, sit on my bed, and put his hand on my forehead. After a few days, he said to me, 'Abani, ask a boon of me.'

"I said, 'Maharaj, please do not come and sit on my bed anymore. You may fall sick.' Hari Maharaj seemed disappointed and said, 'Oh, why do you ask for a thing like that!'

"He continued to come and visit me every day; but he respected my wish and would stand at the open door, inquiring from there how I was getting along.

"After the healing process had begun, I took my first bath in turmeric water, according to the Indian custom. I thought I should bow down to Swami Turiyananda after the bath. But at that stage, when the skin is still scaly, the disease is very contagious; so I bowed down to Hari Maharaj from the door of his room. The upper part of my body was bare. He asked me to come in, but I explained that I did not want to risk infecting anyone. Many devotees were visiting him at the time. He said to me, 'I am ordering you to come in.'

"People moved aside to let me pass, and the swami said, 'Anyone who is afraid of contagion may leave.' No one dared to move. I stepped past the devotees and came to Hari Maharaj's side. He put his hand on my back and said, 'Abani, where is there no contagion? But through Mother's grace, a big rock floats on water; fire loses its power to burn; water loses its power to drench.'"

Three months before Swami Prabhavananda's death, he told this incident for the last time, as well as the following account of his pilgrimage to Kedar-Badri. Then he added, "After I am gone, send these stories to *Prabuddha Bharata* for publication."*

"In 1915, Gurudas Maharaj [later Swami Atulananda] and I were both brahmacharis in Mayavati. Gurudas Maharaj, a Westerner, was about forty-five years old, and I was in my early twenties. He was very devoted to Swami Turiyananda, with whom he had done much traveling.

"Gurudas Maharaj wanted me to make a pilgrimage to Kedarnath and Badrinath with him. I gladly agreed. As he was crippled, he had to be carried the entire way in a *dandi*, a kind of chair carried by two people on each side.

"At Kankhal we stayed in the monastery of the Ramakrishna Order. I walked faster than the people who carried the dandi and arrived at the next stop, Hardwar, before Gurudas Maharaj. I thought I would save him money by doing some cooking myself, so I got fuel and various kinds of foodstuff. There was an inn where pilgrims could stay without paying. I tried

* They were published in *Prabuddha Bharata in* 1978 and 1979, respectively.

to start a fire in one of the rooms, but the smoke was so thick that I had to keep running out of the room. An old widow, who was seated nearby, was watching me. She said, 'Son, have you ever cooked before?'

"'No, Mother.'

"'Do you mind if I prepare the food for you?'

"'Oh no, Mother, please go ahead!'

"So she prepared the meal. First she fed Gurudas Maharaj and me and then the people who carried the dandi. Afterward she also ate.

"After this experience, Gurudas Maharaj suggested, 'Let us hire a cook and also someone to carry our bedding and other things.' That was done.

"We crossed the bridge [probably Lakshman Jhula at Hrishi-kesh], and after ten or fifteen miles we stopped at an inn for the night. I was not used to the altitude and the cold weather, and when I first tried to get up I felt dizzy. But then I became accli-mated, and we began to walk. We walked about fifteen miles and then arrived at an inn. There we had every comfort, and we slept well.

"First we made the trip to Kedarnath, which is at an altitude of eleven thousand feet. You cannot stay there overnight be-cause it is so cold. In the Himalayas eleven thousand feet is not like in America. There is eternal snow and ice. On the way we came upon a holy river that was frozen, so we could walk on it. The path up one steep mountainside was ten miles long. I went slowly, step by step. And I saw that many pilgrims were gasp-ing for breath and had to sit down and rest.

"At Kedarnath Lord Shiva's temple, there is a wonderful at-mosphere. We had no difficulty taking Gurudas Maharaj inside. As he was a Westerner, we had thought the priests might ob-ject. But we were told, 'No, there is no objection here.' So we went in and offered our worship.

"Afterward, a priest fried some puris [bread] for us and gave us molasses, as nothing could be boiled at such an altitude. That same day we came back about ten miles. There is a beauti-ful inn and also a small pool [Gaurikund] where hot and cold springs mix together. You can bathe there. And the water is so hot that you can make a cup of tea, which we did. I bathed in the pool, and it took away all my aches and pains.

"Then we went on our way to Badri Narayan. Coming up one mountainside, I recognized one of Maharaj's disciples. He was senior to me and later came with me to America, where he stayed only four years. His name was Sitapati Maharaj, later Swami Raghavananda. He had come up the mountain from a hospital down below. He was very ill. A brahmachari by the name of Tarasar was with him, but when Sitapati Maharaj saw me, he embraced me and said, 'Brother, don't leave me here. Take me away from this place.' I told him, 'Don't you worry. We will make some arrangement.' Then Gurudas Maharaj's dandi came. We all went down the mountain and hired another dandi for Sitapati Maharaj. So we began our pilgrimage with two and ended up with four.

"One day I went to the river. While I was washing myself, I saw a swami from another order. Suddenly he slipped and fell into the water. The current of the river was very strong. I threw the end of my wet cloth to him, but before he could grasp it, he was smashed against the rocks and was gone. That was quite a shock for me.

"We took the path to Badri Narayan, which is at an altitude of ten thousand feet. Sitapati Maharaj was able to walk now, so the three of us walked, and Gurudas Maharaj was carried in a dandi.

"A narrow path led up the mountain. Down below, the river was flowing with a very strong current. I was walking in front, and right behind me was Gurudas Maharaj, then Sitapati Maharaj, and behind him the other brahmachari. All of a sudden an avalanche came roaring down the mountain. We were all sure we were going to die. I looked back at Gurudas Maharaj. There was a beautiful smile on his face. That gave me such encouragement. The big rocks did not actually touch me, but I could feel the rush of air as they fell just past me. And then, through the Lord's grace, the avalanche suddenly stopped. All the pilgrims sat down and began to chant the Lord's praises.

"Then we walked again. First, we crossed a bridge. There were big mountains before us. The sun was rising. It was such a beautiful sight. All the pilgrims sat down and closed their eyes. Instead of seeing the beauty outside, they thought of the even greater beauty within and began to meditate.

"Again we went on. Finally we arrived at Badri Narayan. All the pilgrims sat down, waiting for the temple to open. We too were seated to one side.

"A bright-looking young priest, about twenty to twenty-four years old, beckoned to me. He said, 'Ask your friends to come and follow me.' He took us to a side of the temple where it was not crowded. When he opened the temple door, some other pilgrims wanted to enter also, but he told them, 'No, it is not for you.' The four of us went in with him, and he closed the door behind us.

"But here is the peculiar thing. Generally a priest stands to one side or in front, facing the deity. But this priest stood in line with the deity, facing us, which is never done. We stayed and looked and had our darshan. After a few minutes, the priest asked, 'Have you had enough darshan?' We came out, but the priest did not leave the temple. He closed the door behind us.

"Again we were seated with the pilgrims. Another man beckoned to me, 'Ask your friends to come with me. The head priest wants to see you.'

"We went, and the head priest with great courtesy made us sit by him. He asked in Hindi about Gurudas Maharaj, 'To what race does this man belong?' I knew a little Hindi, and I answered, 'You have no right to inquire about the race or caste of a monastic.' The head priest replied, 'I know, but does he not come from America?' He explained that he himself did not mind, but as Gurudas Maharaj's skin was white, other people would make trouble for him. If they saw him entering the temple, he would have to pay a large sum of money to have it purified. The head priest asked the three of us not to go into the temple either, as we ate with Gurudas Maharaj. But he was very kind to us. Every hour he would wave the *arati* lights [butter wicks] before the deity and would let us watch from the open temple door. At that time he would not permit other pilgrims to enter the temple. After we had our darshan, he would allow the other pilgrims to go inside. We never told him or anyone else there that we had already been inside the temple.

"For three days and three nights the four of us were practically guests of the head priest. He arranged for our stay in a heated room and sent us the best temple prasad.

"There were about seven or eight priests at Badri Narayan, and we met them all; but we never saw the young priest again who had conducted us into the temple when we first arrived.

"From Badri Narayan, on the way back to Mayavati, Sitapati Maharaj, Guradas Maharaj, and I stopped at Almora, where Swami Turiyananda was then staying in the Ramakrishna Kutir. We did not know where in Almora the kutir was located. Although we had only been told that it was somewhere beside the road, we happened to come to just the right place. I had begun to call loudly, 'Swami Turiyanandaji Maharaj, Swami Turiyanandaji Maharaj!' It was early in the morning. The swami had been warming himself by a fire, dressed only in a *kaupin* [loincloth]. As soon as he heard my voice, he came running outside into the cold to meet me. Think of his love! Then he took me by the hand and led me to the kutir, and Gurudas Maharaj and Sitapati Maharaj also came. He gave us a warm room.

"We stayed with Swami Turiyananda for three days, and we told him the story of our pilgrimage. When he heard about our first darshan at Badri Narayan, when the young priest had taken us inside the temple, he became excited and exclaimed, 'You foolish boys, don't you realize that it was the Lord himself who came in this garb and took you inside? Didn't you recognize him?'"

Commenting on his experience at Badri Narayan, Swami Prabhavananda said, "Yes, the Lord comes down. He has love for all mankind. But only a few recognize that love."

Regarding his visit to Swami Turiyananda in Almora, Swami Prabhavananda added: "When I came to Almora after visiting Kedarnath and Badri Narayan, I stayed for a few days with Swami Turiyananda. He told me this story:

"While he was at Shanti Ashram* he became very discouraged. There was no water. They [a small band of Western students] had to carry water from a distance. And there were poisonous snakes, but they had vowed not to kill anything on the grounds. After staying at Shanti Ashram for almost a year, he returned to India. But before leaving the ashrama, he saw Thakur appear to him in vision, holding his hand and saying, 'Don't leave. I will build a city for you here, and you will do much good for the people of this country.' Then Swami Turiyananda told me, 'But unfortunately I disobeyed him, and look what is happening to me now. I am always sick.'†

"Swami Turiyananda wanted to return to America, but the woman on whom he depended for sending the money was killed in an auto accident. Her name was Shraddha."

———

During his stay in Mayavati, Swami Prabhavananda was assistant editor of *Prabuddha Bharata*. He translated into English one-third of Sarat Chakravarty's conversations with Swamiji, subsequently published by Advaita Ashrama. He also translated into English verses 31–100 of Bhartrihari's *Hundred Verses on Renunciation*. "I remained there for two years," Swami said, referring to Mayavati. "But I was feeling very lonely for Maharaj, so I told the abbot that I wanted to return to him." When Swami wrote to Maharaj about his feelings, Maharaj answered, "All right, come!"

Swami Prabhavananda went directly to Puri where Maharaj was staying at the time. He spent about a month with him. During this period, the annual Car Festival was celebrated by drawing the image of Jagannath in a large chariot through the streets.

"Maharaj, Swami Turiyananda, and all of us went to take part in the festival," Swami Prabhavananda recalled. "It was

* A Vedanta retreat in San Antonio Valley, California.
† Since Swami Prabhavananda heard this story directly from Swami Turiyananda, we have published it here exactly as he used to recount it for the reader's consideration. However, it is important to note that the swami's memory of it differs from two published accounts: the first, which appeared in *Prabuddha Bharata* (January 1925, p. 2) and was later reprinted in Swami Ritajananda's book: *Swami Turiyananda* (Madras: Sri Ramakrishna Math, 1973), p. 83.

a hot summer day, and we took shelter under the huge gate of a house near the temple. Maharaj had been joking with us, but as the time approached to draw the car of Jagannath he became very serious. It seemed that he actually saw the Lord seated in the chariot. His face flushed with ecstasy. Removing his upper garment in a gesture of humility, he took one of the ropes. Swami Turiyananda took the rope next to him, and the rest of us followed their example and joined the crowd in pulling the chariot for some time."

According to Swami Prabhavananda's reminiscences of this period in Puri, one day a rich landowner, a devotee of Maharaj, gave money to feed the untouchables with Jagannath prasad. "Maharaj asked us to make the arrangements," Swami told us. "Several monks of the order, Swami Shankarananda among them, went to supervise. All of us watched the untouchables eat. They were very dirty and sick, but I took a grain of rice from their leavings and ate it. I wanted to test myself.

"Puri is a powerful place. Sri Ramakrishna never went there. He was afraid that if he went he would leave his body. That temple is one of the most potent."

While Swami Prabhavananda was in Puri, several women devotees wanted him to get Maharaj's permission to take them to meet Shankara, the head of the Shankara order in Puri. Swami had gone to see Shankara when he was a boy of fourteen. When Maharaj heard the request, he told Swami, "Ah, Shankara will give you liberation! Go and make japa!" So the women devotees left, and Swami went to make japa.

It was around this time that Maharaj began to discipline Swami Prabhavananda, as Swami used to recall. "The first two years after I joined the order Maharaj didn't scold. Then the first time was in Puri. Swami Shankarananda, Maharaj's private secretary, gave me a receipt one morning and said, 'Go to the railway station.' I didn't inquire into the details. Then I wondered what to do. I happened to meet the young brahmachari who ordinarily handled these matters. He told me, 'Give the receipt to the stationmaster, and when the package comes he will send it. That is all.' So I did that and left, not realizing that the main purpose for the errand was to pick up a special package of fresh fish that had arrived from Calcutta for Maharaj.

"On my return to the ashrama I saw Maharaj, Swami Turiyananda, and Swami Shankarananda waiting. They asked me, 'Where is the fish?'

"'Fish?' Of course, I was empty-handed. Then Swami Shankarananda got a carriage and went to get the fish. All afternoon Maharaj scolded me."*

During Swami Prabhavananda's stay in Puri, Maharaj showed his compassion to Swami's family. Swami occasionally related the circumstances:

"One day I was seated in a corner of the monastery hall, reading Shankara's *Crest-Jewel of Discrimination*, while Maharaj was walking up and down. He looked at me with such affection. The next day I got a letter from my mother saying that my father had died. I read her letter to Maharaj. He said, 'You are a brahmachari. You don't have to observe any *shraddha* ceremonies.'†

"Maharaj gave me his prasad and the prasad from the temple. After three days he said to me, 'What, are you still here? Go and see your mother!' He asked Swami Shankarananda to buy some prasad from the Jagannath Temple and to get a ticket for me. He even had him put me on the train. And so I went. My youngest brother, Arabinda, who was only twelve years old, met me at the station in Vishnupur. We cycled to Khatra, where my father had practiced law, my brother standing behind me on the bicycle holding the basket of prasad. My mother, brothers, and sisters had all been grieving. My mother afterward told me that when she saw me, all her grief left her. Maharaj had sent something for them with me, which all my relatives felt.

"Later I thought that the day Maharaj had looked at me so compassionately, he gave liberation to my father."

After Swami Prabhavananda left his family, he went to visit Swami Premananda in Calcutta. It was their last meeting, which Swami Prabhavananda often described in later years.

* The remainder of this first disciplining is told in *The Eternal Companion*, 3rd edition, Vedanta Press, 73–74.
† Traditionally Hindus observe certain customs when mourning, such as eating only one meal a day cooked by oneself, sleeping on the ground, etc.

"During my last visit with Swami Premananda, he was very ill. He had black fever, for which there was no cure. He was then living at the home of Balaram Bose in Calcutta. Swami Premananda asked me to stay there with him and to assist Swami Saradananda in the secretarial work of the order. Of course, I was very happy at this suggestion. But when I reached Belur Math, I found a letter from Maharaj, saying, 'As soon as you receive this letter, come to Puri. Go to the Udbodhan Office, get however much money is needed, and come by second-class train.' So I went to the Udbodhan and read the letter to Swami Premananda. He told me, 'Write to Maharaj that you can't go to Puri, that you are staying here.'

"'How can I do that?' I asked Swami Premananda. Maharaj was my guru and, moreover, president of the order.

"Swami Premananda's temper was rising. 'What, you won't obey me?' he asked.

"'But, sir, when it comes to obeying you or Maharaj, I must obey Maharaj!' This answer irritated him all the more. 'Get out of my sight,' he exclaimed. 'I can't look at you!'

"Somehow Swami Premananda's anger did not affect me. Deep in my heart I knew that he was just acting, and that his plans for me had been prompted by his love. But I left him because he was sick, and I did not want to excite him unduly. I went downtown to do some errands before my trip to Puri.

"In the meantime Swami Premananda had sent for me. As soon as I returned to the Udbodhan, some of the boys told me, 'You had better go upstairs. Swami Premananda is waiting for you.' I went to his room. He had ordered my favorite sweets and cool water, and he asked me to sit in front of him and eat and drink. He would not let me go. Then he inquired, 'Are you angry with me?'

"'Why should I be angry with you, sir?'

"'Because I scolded you.'

"'But, sir, your scolding was a blessing!' That was how I really felt. Then Swami Premananda said, 'Well, this is the last time you see me. We shall all be gone, and you boys will have to take charge of the mission work. I wanted you to learn these duties from Swami Saradananda, but it seems that Maharaj has other plans for you. So go to Maharaj!' His mood changed. Like a little boy he said, 'But don't tell Maharaj that I scolded you!' Then he asked me to send him some holy water from the Jagannath Temple in Puri.

"The morning I arrived in Puri, I sat at the feet of Maharaj, and he inquired about Swami Premananda. I told Maharaj that he was very ill. Then Maharaj talked for a long time about how emotional Swami Premananda was. When he was in East Bengal, many Muslims began to follow him. This angered the Muslim priest. He taunted Swami Premananda one day, 'You tell us that all religions are true, and that all is One. Can you eat with me?' The Muslim priest bit into a mango and then handed the mango to Swami Premananda. Sri Ramakrishna had forbidden Swami Premananda to eat any impure food because his body was so pure, but he disobeyed and ate the mango. Then he fell ill.

"Suddenly Maharaj inquired, 'Did he ask anything of you?'

"'Yes, Maharaj, he asked for some holy water.'

"Then the thunder fell. 'What! Such a great soul asked such a small thing of you, and you kept quiet so long! Do you know how great he is? Whichever direction he looks, that entire direction becomes purified.'

"Maharaj immediately ordered his secretary to get some holy water from the Jagannath Temple to send to his brother-disciple."

Swami Prabhavananda has related that Swami Premananda's last words were "Grace, grace, grace." The swami entered mahasamadhi [final state of transcendence at death] in July 1918.

Shortly after Swami Prabhavananda returned to Puri, Maharaj decided to send him to Madras. Before leaving for Madras, Swami asked Maharaj, "Won't you give me *sannyas* [final monastic vows] before I go?" Maharaj replied, "Why didn't you ask me a few days back? Now it is too late. Everything has been arranged."

Maharaj made special arrangements for Swami to travel to Madras. In Swami's own words: "I was a young brahmachari. Maharaj didn't want me to make the train journey from Puri to Madras without a break. First he asked his private secretary to buy a second-class ticket for me to Madras. Then he told him, 'Send a telegram to Keshab Murti [a devotee] in Coconada, and say that this boy must rest there because he cannot travel all the way from here to Madras at a stretch.' His secretary objected that since I had come all the way from Mayavati to Puri, I could travel from Puri to Madras without breaking the journey. Maharaj said to him, 'You don't understand. This journey is difficult.' So the telegram was sent.

"A telegram came from the devotee in confirmation, saying he would welcome me. One hour later Maharaj asked, 'What was in that telegram?' I got the name mixed up. Maharaj said somewhat sarcastically, 'Ah, your intelligence is like that of Brihaspati [the guru of the gods]!' Then I got the telegram and read it to him. Keshab Murti had arranged for me to stay with him for three days. As the Madras Mail train did not normally stop in Coconada, his brother, Surya Narayan, who was a very prominent man in the legislative council, sent a telegram to the governor. The governor sent a telegram to the superintendent of the railway, and the superintendent of the railway, in turn, arranged to have the Madras Mail deposit me in Coconada on a particular day and, again, stop to take me to Madras.

"When I got down from the Madras Mail in Coconada, Keshab Murti was waiting for me with his carriage. He had a house for me, and he had engaged a special cook because he knew that Bengalis couldn't stand the extremely hot chilies used in South Indian cooking. But the first bite of the special 'mild' cooking burnt all the way down. After three days, Keshab Murti put me on the train for Madras."

Swami used to tell the story of Maharaj's special arrangements for his trip to Madras in order to illustrate Maharaj's loving concern for him—like that of a parent for his little child.

Plate 3. Swami Brahmananda, Kashimpur, 1916

CHAPTER FOUR

From Madras to Calcutta

SWAMI PRABHAVANANDA SPENT four years at the Madras monastery, the oldest and most influential center of the Ramakrishna Order in South India. One of his duties as a young brahmachari, was to wash the marble floor of the beautiful large shrine room and to clean and polish the brass vessels used in the worship.

During his stay in Madras, Swami was given responsibilities of a literary nature. He translated into English *Saint Durgacharan Nag*, a biography of Ramakrishna's great householder-disciple Nag Mahashay, which was originally written in Bengali by Sarat Chandra Chakravarty, a disciple of Swamiji.

Swami also edited *The Vedanta Kesari*, a monthly magazine published by the Madras math.* In connection with his efforts to obtain a contribution to the *Kesari* from Swami Shivananda, he used to tell the following story: "One day I requested Swami Shivananda to write an article for the magazine. He said he would. I bought a new notebook and a new pen for him for this purpose. After two weeks I inquired if he had written anything. Swami Shivananda said, 'Abani, I want to write something, and I thought of a subject. But as soon as I thought of the subject, I immediately came to the conclusion. So what could I write?'"

* Officially known today as Sri Ramakrishna Math, Chennai.

Swami Ramakrishnananda had founded the Madras math in 1897, approximately twenty years before Swami arrived there. He served as its head until he passed away in 1911.

Swami occasionally related anecdotes pertaining to Swami Ramakrishnananda and the early days of the order:

"Once a Vaishnava pundit came to the Madras center and gave a lecture. It became very long, and after an hour or so Swami Ramakrishnananda asked him to stop. This offended the pundit. Later he sent the message that he would forgive Swami Ramakrishnananda, but his Krishna could never forgive him. To this, Swami Ramakrishnananda sent back the reply, 'My Krishna will teach your Krishna a lesson.'"

One story that took place during a visit by Swami Brahmananda to Madras math shows that even his brother disciples sometimes underestimated his spiritual power.

"Maharaj had a disciple who took care of him for a long time. This disciple contracted smallpox [in Madras] and was sent to a hospital. Swami Ramakrishnananda used to go and visit the disciple there, and the disciple pleaded with Swami Ramakrishnananda, 'Please ask Maharaj to come just once and stand at the door. I want to look at his face once more before I die.' Every day Swami Ramakrishnananda begged Maharaj to go to the hospital, but Maharaj didn't answer him. The disciple died. Then Swami Ramakrishnananda burst out, 'Maharaj, you are very cruel.'

"'Why?'

"'This boy served you, and he wanted to see you just once more, for a moment, and you didn't go.'

Then Maharaj said, 'How do you know that I did not go?'"

————

Most of Swami Prabhavananda's reminiscences of his stay in Madras are linked to his memories of Maharaj.

"I remember that the day Maharaj arrived at the Madras math, Baradananda, one of his attendants, sang this song: 'All our sorrow has dissolved in joy.' That song expressed our feeling perfectly." Swami Prabhavananda loved this song and in later years used to request to hear it when Bengali singers came to the Hollywood center. The song is given below in Swami Ashokananda's translation from the Bengali:

All my sorrow has been lifted by seeing thee.
What boundless grace is thine!
My heart has drunk pure nectar and is soothed.
When I do not have thee, all things seem empty,
   and the sun, the moon, and the stars lose their light.

O companion of my soul, there is none like thee;
An ocean of love swells within when I remember thee.
Stay thou with me day and night
   that my life may have its Lord;
And keep me ever in the shadow of thy feet—
   in life and in death.

"The day Maharaj arrived in Madras, I massaged him for a long time. It was very hot, and I was perspiring. About three hours passed, and I was tired. I thought Maharaj had gone to sleep and stopped massaging him. Just then he opened his eyes. He realized my embarrassment at having stopped massaging without his order and made no mention of it. He just asked me to get him some tobacco.

"When I massaged Maharaj, I would get a fragrance. It was wonderful. I would not wash my hands for some time.

"One time I wiped Maharaj's feet with the *chaddar* [prayer shawl] I was wearing.

"Maharaj was a big man—tall and strong. He had been an athlete in his youth. His skin was soft, but when he stiffened his muscles he was like iron.

"Swami Turiyananda said to me once that Maharaj's back looked like the back of Sri Ramakrishna."

Swami Prabhavananda used to impress on his disciples that Maharaj was much more than an enlightened guru, that even among the ever-free souls he was considered as someone special. Swami quoted Swamiji as saying about Maharaj, "I try to grasp ... but I can only go so far. I can't circumscribe him." The love and respect of these two great disciples of Sri Ramakrishna was reciprocal, as described in *The Eternal Companion.*

On the subject of Maharaj, Swami Prabhavananda once wrote in a letter: "Maharaj was not an ordinary illumined soul. He lived twenty-four hours a day in union with God. What he spoke came directly from God. There was no separate individuality left in him. He was one with God. As you sat in his presence, you were in the living presence of God. He would raise the consciousness of those near him, and there was a feeling of ineffable joy. You felt that it was so easy to experience God. No mere saint could do what he did silently."

One day Swami said about Maharaj, "We were in love with him. Maharaj was our father, mother, and everything. When you were with him, you felt you were with God. You could not think of lust in his presence. Of course, we were used to his atmosphere. But when we came away, we felt other places were dry. However, it is also true that you carried his presence with you."

When Swami Prabhavananda was asked whether he was always aware that Maharaj was one with God, he answered, "There was always an undercurrent. When we came out of his room, we thought, 'Ah!' But while we were with him, he would joke and make us forget who he was; otherwise we could not have approached him and served him."

Who was Maharaj? The following incident relating to this question probably took place in Madras or in Calcutta. Swami Prabhavananda, who was present, recalled the conversation:

"A young boy once came to see Maharaj, and he was seated next to him. Ramlal Dada was also present. I was standing near Maharaj. The young boy asked, 'Maharaj, please tell us who you really are.' Maharaj said, 'How should I know? Ask Ramlal Dada.' Ramlal Dada in turn said, 'No, you ask Maharaj.' This exchange went on several times. Meanwhile, I was thinking to myself, 'Why all this botheration about who Maharaj really is? All we need to know is that Maharaj is simply our Maharaj.'

Maharaj surmised my thought and with a smile turned to me. I felt that he was going to ask me what I thought of him. To avoid this, I turned and quietly slipped away."

Maharaj could recognize at a glance the spiritual condition of anyone with whom he came in contact. Swami Prabhavananda used to tell the following story about one of his roommates in Madras: "An old, retired man came to our monastery and said, 'I want to live here. Give me a room and some food. That is all I need.' He handed everything he owned over to the abbot. One day he confided to me that he had lived a very wayward life.

"When Maharaj came to our monastery after a few years, he saw this old man and asked, 'Where did you find this *rishi* [seer, sage]?' The old man stayed in the same room with me, and I noticed that he would wake up at three o'clock in the morning, sit within his mosquito net with his beads, and continue to make japa with such regularity that he put us boys to shame."

Knowing Maharaj's deep insight into people's character, Swami Sharvananda, his disciple and head of the Madras math, once asked Maharaj, "What do you think of Gandhi?" Swami Prabhavananda recalled that Maharaj answered in English, "Through sheer force of ethical life he is knocking at the highest door of spirituality."

Maharaj knew the motives of those who wished to meet him before they came into his presence. Swami Prabhavananda related: "Maharaj would know ahead of time who would come to see him. If he didn't want to see someone, he would actually get a fever and would tell us, 'I don't feel good; I can't see anyone.'"

Unless an aspirant approaches a guru in a spirit of humility, spiritual efforts are fruitless. Swami gave the following example: "A young man wanted initiation from Maharaj in a forced way. Maharaj told him to wait, but the man said that he would fast until death if he were not initiated by Maharaj. He began to fast. Then he was brought to our ashrama. Maharaj said that he should break his fast. I saw the man dying. Maharaj did not go to see him. This man was not willing to obey Maharaj."

There were instances of persons who came to Maharaj after having a spiritual experience. Swami Prabhavananda wrote in *The Eternal Companion:*

"At one time Sri Ramakrishna appeared in a dream to two ladies belonging to an aristocratic family and told them to visit Maharaj. They had never heard of Sri Ramakrishna nor read anything about him. But they went to Maharaj and were initiated by him." Swami told us the same incident in more detail, identifying persons and places: "The wife of the Maharaja of Cochin and her sister never went outside their palace. Once the Maharani had a vision of Sri Ramakrishna in which Thakur told her, 'Go to my son Rakhal.' Maharaj was staying at the Madras math at the time. The two ladies secretly left the palace and came to the monastery at Madras. As soon as they arrived, a telegram was sent to the palace so that the Maharaja would not worry about them. After Maharaj talked to the Maharani and her sister, he said to me, 'We think we have to preach the Lord. But you see, the Lord does his own preaching. Be the witness.'"

Swami Prabhavananda told us that Maharaj rarely spoke of his personal relationship with Sri Ramakrishna. After saying this, Swami proceeded to relate the following incident without identifying the location where it took place: "Many years after Sri Ramakrishna's passing away, Pulin Mitra, a disciple of Swamiji, was present at a celebration of Thakur's birthday. Pulin was seated by Maharaj and was singing and accompanying himself on the tanpura [a long-necked string instrument]. At that time Maharaj had a vision of Thakur standing near the instrument and then said, 'Whosoever will take the name of my Thakur today, knowingly or unknowingly, will attain liberation.' That was the only time anyone heard Maharaj use the words 'my Thakur.' And so many people took the name of the Lord that day!"

Maharaj would frequently inquire into his disciples' spiritual practices. One day in Madras he asked Swami Prabhavananda, "What are you studying now?" Swami answered, "The *Yoga Sutras*." Maharaj commented, "Very good." When relating this conversation to his own disciples, Swami added, "Scriptural study is very important."

Maharaj recommended spiritual practices to his disciples according to their tendencies. Swami recalled, "When I was in Puri with Maharaj, before he sent me to Madras, he asked me to repeat Shiva prayers every morning.

"In Madras, Maharaj asked me to go to the Shiva temple* to offer worship every Monday for one year. One day he gave me money and said, 'Go do the Shiva puja in my name.' The offering was half a coconut with ashes. I brought it back after the worship and left it in a box for prasad. When I prostrated before Maharaj, he asked me, 'Where is the prasad?' I got it. He said, 'Touch it to my forehead.' Coconut shells are rough. With great care I touched the shell to his forehead."

Swami said that Maharaj told him once, "Shiva lives in the beads."

Regarding Maharaj's instructions to him on meditation, Swami said, "Once Maharaj asked me to do *purascharana* [performing japa a certain number of times each day, methodically increasing and decreasing the amount] for one year. Otherwise he never asked me to meditate. He told me only, 'Abani, love me.' He repeated this three times. He gave me everything."

In *The Eternal Companion* Swami Prabhavananda quotes Maharaj's reference to the grace of the guru, the grace of the Lord, the grace of the Lord's devotees, and the grace of one's own mind. Swami one day remarked to his disciples, "Maharaj was playing with us like children. He used to tell us, 'You have to have the grace of the guru.' I should have said to him, 'Maharaj, but the guru gives one the grace of one's own mind.'"

In Madras, Swami Prabhavananda underwent intensive discipline from Maharaj. Many instances are described in *The Eternal Companion*. Recalling this period of his life in later years, Swami sometimes added details to the stories:

---

* The Shiva temple in Mylapore, Madras, to which Swami used to go, is within a couple of blocks of the Madras math. It is known as the Kapaleeswara Temple. Kapaleeswara means "Lord of Fate" and is an epithet of Shiva.

"When Maharaj came to Madras, he began to discipline me. It went on for three months. He disciplined me in a very interesting way.

"For three months he scolded me, whether I was sitting or standing. Even when I was in my bed at night he would send for me, 'Bring that boy from Vishnupur!' So in that way Vishnupur is blessed.

"When Maharaj scolded, he gave one the power to bear it. And I was a boy whom my parents were careful not to scold. I could not stand harsh words. And with Maharaj—I myself was surprised. I never reacted with resentment.

"When Maharaj scolded me, I never defended myself. There was a disciple who did; that was the end of him. Once Maharaj said to him, 'What a dumbbell you are!' He answered, 'No, Maharaj, I'm not a dumbbell. I am a university graduate.' Maharaj folded his palms and said to him, 'Oh, forgive me.' That was the end of that boy.

"Sometimes Maharaj would rebuke us severely when we felt completely innocent, or he would scold us for what seemed like very insignificant reasons. Of course, we never argued with Maharaj, because he would make us understand that there were deeper reasons for his discipline than the apparent grounds on which he was reproaching us. But there was always an undercurrent of joy.

"Maharaj used to rebuke us for things we had not done. Once I was supposed to have some letterheads designed for Maharaj. I brought him a book of typefaces, and he chose an ornamental font that showed a little gap in the S. I read the proofs carefully. Gopal, who later became Swami Siddheswarananda, picked up the finished letterheads from the printer and took them to Maharaj. Maharaj became agitated and told him, 'Call that boy from Vishnupur! He doesn't know how to read proofs.' Gopal came trembling and said, 'Maharaj says the S is broken.' I went to Maharaj, and he scolded me vehemently. I opened the stylebook. The S showed a little space that was part of the design. He took the stylebook from my hands, threw it on the floor, and went on scolding me.

"One day I was standing beside the doorsill. I knew better than to stand on it.* Maharaj was watching me. He could see that I was not moving, but he said sarcastically, 'Look at that boy! His intelligence is like that of Brihaspati!' He kept right on scolding me for standing on the doorsill."

After three months of scolding by Maharaj in Madras, Swami Prabhavananda thought he had lost his guru's love. He wrote in *The Eternal Companion*, "Because I could not endure the thought, that very night I decided to run away from the monastery and hide myself forever."

Many years later, describing his state of mind, Swami confided, "One morning, not sleeping at all during the night, I decided to go to the ocean and drown myself. But first I went to prostrate before Maharaj and mentally said goodbye to him." Then the incident continued as described in *The Eternal Companion*, with Maharaj telling Swami to sit down and continuing to scold him for a while before reassuring him at the end of their meeting, "Our love is so deep that we do not let you know how much we love you."

Swami Prabhavananda recalled receiving special affection from Maharaj's brother-disciples on occasions when Maharaj was disciplining him. "When Maharaj was very hard on me, what love Swami Shivananda and Swami Turiyananda showed me! They were more than family."

One day Maharaj gave Swami an extraordinary teaching on the relationship between morality and spirituality. Swami said about himself: "I was puritanical. One of the brothers did something, and I did not like it. Maharaj called me aside and said, 'Look here—what is morality? If one has devotion, morality and purity will follow without one even trying to be moral or pure.'" After quoting Maharaj's statement, Swami was concerned that people might misunderstand this truth, and he added, "How can I teach this?"

Although Swami told us that he never argued with Maharaj in order to defend himself, there were a few occasions when he

---

* In India it is considered inauspicious to stand on the doorsill.

answered back to him: "A few times I talked back to Maharaj. That brought out something from him."

In one case, partially described in *The Eternal Companion*, Swami related the circumstances to us in greater detail:

"Maharaj sent me to Madras and then he came to visit. There my scolding began, lasting three months. I didn't write to him for a month when he went to Bangalore. When he came back, he said, 'Come with me to the garden.' He saw what I had planted. Then he asked, 'Why didn't you write to me?'

"'Oh, you got all news of me from Mahapurush Maharaj.'

"Maharaj said sarcastically, 'So you have got the key to the treasury and don't care for me any more!'

"'Yes, Maharaj, you keep the key in your own hands and you talk to me like that!' Maharaj didn't say anything. He came and sat down. I sat at his feet, and then he began to scold me. It was my mistake. I should have written to him and told him that I wanted to be with him in Bangalore, but I didn't. I couldn't understand then. Now I can. I should have accompanied him to Bangalore, or at least I should have written a letter saying that I would have liked to come there. But I had wounded vanity."

Swami Prabhavananda used to recall another occasion when he talked back to Maharaj: "Maharaj had been saying, 'I can accept and I can reject, as I have rejected [X].' I shook my finger at Maharaj and said, 'Maharaj, I believe every word that you say, but not this. You have not given up [X], and you can never give him up.' Maharaj relaxed and smiled."

On two occasions, both times in Madras, Swami Prabhavananda saw Maharaj in samadhi. The first time Maharaj had been invited by an old sadhu who had about two dozen young nuns under him. The nuns were going to dance. Swami related, "Maharaj was seated on a chair, Swami Shivananda on his right and Ramlal Dada on his left. I was seated in front of them, on the ground.

"Maharaj teased Ramlal Dada. He asked him in Bengali, 'Which one do you prefer?'

"Before the dance began, one nun came with a bowl of perfumed water. She dipped Maharaj's feet in the water and then dried his feet with her hair. Then the nuns danced with sticks in their hands, beating time to the music. They sang:

Drink this milk, my Lord Gopala,
Drink this milk, O son of Nanda,
This sweet milk, I, Namadeva,
Bring you in this bowl of gold.

"While they sang, Maharaj went into deep samadhi. Four nuns at a time took turns approaching Maharaj while the others were singing and dancing. Each nun who approached him wiped Maharaj's feet with her hair and offered him milk to drink. As Maharaj was in samadhi, the milk ran down his chin. Each nun gave him milk and wiped his chin with a cloth. It took a long time, perhaps an hour.

"The second time I saw Maharaj in samadhi was in front of the Madras math. Maharaj was going to be photographed. In those days they had old-fashioned cameras. The photographer had to put his head under a cloth and focus the picture. A cot was brought outdoors for Maharaj to sit on to get enough light. Swami Sharvananda was fussing how Maharaj should sit. Maharaj was becoming a bit impatient and noticing that I was standing near him, he suddenly turned to me and said, 'Make me sit the way you would like it.' I took his legs and crossed them. As soon as he was seated in that posture, he went into samadhi" [plate 4].

During the time of the Durga Puja and Kali Puja observances in the fall of 1921, Swami received his final vows as well as his sannyas name from Maharaj. Swami has told us that *Prabhavananda* means "He whose bliss is in the Source" or "in the Creator of the Universe." For sannyas Swami observed the traditional complete fast and did not smoke.

Within a short time, Swami Sharvananda had some plans for the new sannyasi. Swami Prabhavananda related:

"After Maharaj gave me sannyas, Swami Sharvananda wanted me to go to Colombo and take charge of the center there. Every other time Maharaj accepted his suggestions. This time

Sharvananda begged Maharaj, but Maharaj did not listen. He knew I was to come to this country [America]."

As already mentioned, Swami Prabhavananda told us that during the scolding period in Madras, Maharaj referred to him as "that boy from Vishnupur." Swami also said that when the scolding stopped, "then it was nothing but affection." When Maharaj showed Swami affection, he called him "Khoka," which means "Baby."

"We were then on very affectionate terms. One day Maharaj was seated on a chair, and I was sitting cross-legged in front of him. His feet were resting on my knees, and I was massaging them. He made me talk freely, but I can't remember a word I said. I don't know whether I was in a normal state of consciousness or not. I spoke maybe for half an hour or an hour. I recall only the last sentence, in which I addressed him as *tumi* [the Bengali form of "you," which is used for a friend or an equal]. I recall this because Maharaj leaned forward with an amused smile and asked, 'What did you say?' That made me self-conscious, and I repeated the sentence using *apani* [the respectful form of "you," by which he was addressed]. Then Maharaj appeared to lose interest. He leaned back in the chair and said, 'Oh.'

"Maharaj knew the past, present, and future of each of his disciples. I felt he made me talk in order to corroborate his intuitive knowledge of what was in my subconscious mind." When Swami was asked, "Did you know why Maharaj did that at the time?" he said, "No, not until much later."

In Madras Maharaj gave Swami Prabhavananda a teaching on service that Swami followed till the end of his life. Swami said to a few disciples on Sri Ramakrishna's birthday, March 3, 1976 [only four months before his mahasamadhi]: "Maharaj once told me, 'Wherever you go, stay patiently, bite the earth, and build something for me.'" Swami explained that "to bite the earth" is a Bengali expression that means to stay at all costs; "to build something for me" meant that Maharaj wanted Swami to establish a house for the Lord. Swami added, "You cannot establish anything unless you give your whole life to a place. It is not an easy task."

In a rare statement of self-revelation, Maharaj one day made reference to the parable in *The Gospel of Sri Ramakrishna* of the man with the dye tub who dyed cloth according to the color each person wanted. Swami told us, "Maharaj said, 'I am that dye,' meaning that he could instruct aspirants according to each one's temperament and ideal."

In retrospect, it seemed to Swami that he could hear "the echo of the teachings of Christ" in Maharaj's teachings. One day Swami said about the end of Maharaj's last visit in Madras:

"I knew Maharaj never read the Bible, but Maharaj would quote to me almost word for word what Christ taught. It was about a week before Maharaj left Madras that I was arranging flowers in his room. I did not notice that he had come in. Suddenly he whispered into my ear, 'Lovest thou me?' A thrill passed through my whole being. I could neither speak nor move; I was completely paralyzed. When I was able to turn around and look back, he was already leaving the room. Only much later did I read Christ's words [John 21:15–17] in the Bible."

It was the day of Maharaj's departure for Bhubaneswar. Swami Prabhavananda often spoke of it: "I have already told in *The Eternal Companion* that the last day I spent with Maharaj was when he was leaving Madras. He was walking up and down as I was cooking rice payas [pudding] for him. It was on this occasion that he whispered to me, 'I feel so bad to leave you now.' Then he came back, looked at the payas and told me, 'That is too much sugar.' I said, 'No, Maharaj, that is the right quantity. An expert told me.' But sure enough, it was too sweet."

Before leaving Madras, Maharaj told Swami Prabhavananda that he wanted him to visit places of pilgrimage in South India and afterward join him in Bhubaneswar. Then Maharaj added, "When you come to Bhubaneswar, I will teach you many kinds of spiritual disciplines."

Swami commented, "I made the greatest mistake of my life

in not begging Maharaj to take me to Bhubaneswar with him, because I would have had many opportunities to visit places of pilgrimage in the future."

When Swami arrived in Bhubaneswar after his pilgrimage, Maharaj had left, but there was a letter waiting for him, written by Maharaj's secretary. Maharaj had signed in English in his own hand, "Yours affectionately, Brahmananda." And he had added in Bengali in his own writing, "I miss you very much."

Swami often told us, regretfully, "Even then if I had gone, I would have had the opportunity of seeing him again. But, alas, when I came to Bhubaneswar, he had already left for Calcutta. I never saw him again in his physical body."

————

Maharaj made preparations for his final departure from this world in the early months of 1922. Swamis Sharvananda, Nirvanananda, and Siddheswarananda were among those of his disciples who saw him at Balaram Bose's house and related the events of his last days to Swami Prabhavananda. The moving description of Maharaj's mahasamadhi, written in *The Eternal Companion*, is well known. Swami Prabhavananda sometimes recounted stories of Maharaj's final leave-taking:

"A few days before Maharaj passed away, he said to Surya Maharaj [Swami Nirvanananda], 'I have no more desires left in my mind.' But what desires were in him? Only to help others."

From Swamis Sharvananda and Siddheswarananda, Swami Prabhavananda heard that Maharaj made the following statement on his deathbed: "I am the last bridge that spans the chasm between the known and the unknown, between man and God." Swami explained this meant that Maharaj was the last of the six *ishvarakotis* [ever-free souls] to leave the body.

Another time, when Swami Prabhavananda was speaking to us of Maharaj's last days on earth, he said, "When Maharaj was on his deathbed and his disciples were weeping, he said, 'Do not grieve. I shall be with you always.' His words were like Christ's. He *was* Christ, the Son of God. And Ramakrishna was the source of incarnations—the Mother herself—not just a part, but the whole thing."

Swami Prabhavananda used to tell three more incidents that pertain to the period of his stay in Madras. The first two are connected with the South Indian pilgrimage that he made in accordance with Maharaj's wishes.

"Before leaving on the pilgrimage, I said to the monks at the Madras math, 'Please don't tell anyone that I don't have any money.' I left the monastery with only three rupees. I asked the ticket clerk at the railway station how far three rupees would take me. While he was calculating, a disciple of Maharaj, whom I had met once, pushed me aside from the counter to buy a ticket for me. He was a rich man. He had asked about me at the Madras math and, having found out that I had gone to the railway station, had arrived just in time to buy a ticket for my destination, Rameswaram.

"I stopped in Madurai. A liveried servant told me, 'The district judge is waiting for you.' The district judge became my host. Everywhere I had the best reception. That is how Maharaj kept me all my life. People wanted to give me money. I had left Madras with three rupees. I returned to the Madras math with three hundred rupees and gave a feast for the monastery."

Regarding the second incident of his pilgrimage, Swami related, "While I was going on a pilgrimage to the temple of Shankara in South India, I came upon a huge crowd of untouchables. One of the customs of that part of the country was to shout loudly whenever a caste-Hindu would pass by, because the untouchable had to warn him to keep a distance so he would not become polluted.

"I couldn't bear this. And so when my host, a prominent man of the district, asked if there was anything he could do to be of service to me, I replied, 'Yes, please give these untouchables a big meal, for they look very hungry.' Two days later, preparations were made. Every untouchable was invited, and thousands poured into the grounds. But they would not come near the buildings or the caste-people. I saw this. They were really afraid to come near, so I beckoned, but they only backed off farther. Exasperated because I couldn't speak their language, I just ran up and grabbed the nearest child and hugged him closely to show there was no pollution. The untouchables backed away again in shock and bewilderment. And then all of a sudden, they let up deafening shouts of joy and came forward to have their meal."

The last incident regarding Swami Prabhavananda's stay in Madras took place at a time when Maharaj was not there. It concerns his second experience of taking siddhi, the first having been at Kankhal in 1912. On this second occasion, Swami Sharvananda gave Swami a full glass of siddhi as prasad, not realizing that Swami had already had a cup of it. Swami told us that the first effect of the drug made him feel as if he was going to die. He remembered wanting to die with the Lord's name on his lips, so he chanted "Jaya Sri Ramakrishna," his voice becoming louder and louder. His friend Paresh realized what had happened, took Swami to his room, and poured cold water over him. Swami felt better and sang a devotional song. Then his vision changed, and he saw all the monks lighted and the holy pictures living.

Swami Sharvananda was called. He thought that Swami had lost the balance of his mind and arranged for a doctor to come. The doctor was Swami's friend, but on this occasion Swami could not stand his presence because he saw him as black, not lighted. The doctor gave a prescription and left. Swami became sleepy and asked to use Maharaj's shoes as his pillow. His friend Paresh tied some books together and told Swami they were Maharaj's shoes. Swami was satisfied and went to sleep.

The immediate effect of the drug lasted for three days. While Swami was walking, suddenly the universe seemed to disappear. Swami told us that following this siddhi incident he experienced a period of spiritual dryness for six months.

In later years Swami Prabhavananda explained, not only to his disciples and students, but also in publications and on television, that drug experiences are psychic, not spiritual. He said that there is neither ecstatic bliss nor transformation of character through drugs as there is through spiritual experience. As Swami sometimes expressed it, he was able to speak with authority on this subject, as he himself had had both types of experience, psychic and spiritual.

————————

Swami Prabhavananda used to quote Maharaj as saying about Bhubaneswar that it was "the hidden Banaras." Maharaj himself had arranged the selection of a site for the monastery at Bhubaneswar and had opened the new math in October 1919. When Swami Prabhavananda came to the Ramakrishna Math, Bhubaneswar, he had an experience that convinced him of the efficacy of worship. He told us, "On the third day of performing the ritualistic worship, I did not offer salt to Sri Ramakrishna with the offerings of cucumber and sweets. While making the food offering, it is usual to come out of the shrine, close the doors, and meditate that the Lord is eating. But the day was hot; I was drowsy and lay down. A young brahmin boy with a lighted body appeared to me and said, 'You did not offer Thakur any salt. Thakur cannot take cucumber without salt.' I got up and went to see Swami Atmananda to ask him about it. He said, 'Yes, that is true. Thakur could not eat cucumber without salt. I asked, 'What can be done?' Swami Atmananda advised, 'Take some salt, open the door of the shrine, place the salt on the food tray, and then come out again.' Thus it was proved to me in three days that the Lord accepts what we offer."

Swami Prabhavananda also related another incident that took place in Bhubaneswar: "One day at Bhubaneswar, in the summer, I cooked. All the cooks had left because of the heat. Six or seven of us cooks took turns cooking. When it was my turn, the man in charge of the kitchen said to me, 'I can give you only so much butter. But I leave the key to the storeroom with you.' And so I was able to produce a good meal."

After staying one year at Bhubaneswar, Swami returned to Belur Math. Sometime between 1921 and 1923, he met Swami

Abhedananda, who had recently returned from America. Swami recalled, "Swami Abhedananda was handsome, tall, and well-built. I saw him when he was old. He became fond of me. He used to send for me at the Belur Math."

Swami also met Swami Adbhutananda [Latu Maharaj], probably in the Calcutta area. Swami told us, "I met Latu Maharaj and prostrated before him. Then I went to visit him in his ashrama.* He was talking to himself. I did not understand what he was saying, but I found out that he was talking to the Lord, complaining about his illness."

Swami also related the following incident about Swami Adbhutananda: "At one time several young monks came across a difficult passage in the Upanishads. They could not understand it, although they referred to a number of commentaries. One of them later told me that they went to Latu Maharaj and asked him for an explanation. As Latu Maharaj did not know Sanskrit, they phrased the passage in his own language. He thought for a moment and then exclaimed, 'I've got it!' With a simple illustration he explained the text, and the young monks found wonderful meaning in it."

In 1922 a famous actress who had become a disciple of Maharaj asked to meet Swami Prabhavananda. Swami explained to us that Hindu society used to look down on actresses in India as social outcasts because they were prostitutes or mistresses of wealthy benefactors. Then Swami told us this story:

"Shortly after Maharaj passed away, Tara came to the Belur Math. She had heard that I was a disciple of Maharaj and wished to see me. I did not want to meet her, knowing what kind of a life she had led. But since she was right at the door of my room, I had no way of refusing without hurting her feelings. When I met her on the verandah, she bowed down, untied my shoes, and touched my feet. I felt something pure and soothing in her touch. That taught me a lesson."†

* The first meeting probably occurred during Swami's college years, as Swami Adbhutananda left Calcutta in October 1912 to spend the last eight years of his life in Varanasi, where he stayed in several different places.
† Tara's reminiscences of Maharaj are included in the revised edition of *The Eternal Companion* (Vedanta Press, 1970).

After Maharaj had passed away in April 1922, Swami Shivananda was elected president of the Ramakrishna Math and Mission. Swami Prabhavananda told us:

"Mahapurush Maharaj was the newly appointed president. I took permission from him to go to Almora in the Himalayas to practice austerities. Within a week, Mahapurush Maharaj sent for me and said, 'The swami in the Malaya Straits [Videhananda] wants an assistant. None of the boys wants to go there. Now I am asking you. Will you go?' (My brother-monks had refused because we were all contemporaries of Videhananda.) I said, 'Yes, Maharaj, he is a friend of mine. I will go. But please give me a month's time.' I wanted to go to Banaras and visit Swami Turiyananda before leaving India.

"When I saw Swami Turiyananda and told him that I was being sent to Singapore, he said, 'Give light, and more light will come.' But he did not like the idea of my going to Singapore. He said, 'As long as they are sending you outside of India, why don't they send you to America?' And that is exactly what happened. The plans were later changed, and I was sent to the United States."

Swami Prabhavananda's last darshan of Swami Turiyananda during this visit to Banaras was in June 1922, one month before Swami Turiyananda's mahasamadhi. Swami Prabhavananda told us that at this last meeting Swami Turiyananda reminded him of the first time Swami had massaged his feet:

"Before I joined the monastery, I used to massage Maharaj. After lunch I would go to Swami Turiyananda's room next door and massage him. The first time I went to Swami Turiyananda's room, I just opened the door, went in, and started to massage him. He sat up to see who it was and then lay down and relaxed again. Nothing was said. I continued to massage him and then left."

Their final meeting must have taken place between eight to eleven years later. At that time Swami Turiyananda reminded Swami of that first massage by disclosing to him, "I knew that first time that you had a power in you." Swami reminisced: "He also told me he knew that I belonged to them, and said many other nice things. When I protested, 'Maharaj, I am not any of these things you say I am,' he replied, 'What do you know about yourself? I see not what you are, but what you are going to become.'

"I remember his affection. He was very ill and could hardly move. After I said goodbye to him, he turned his head and continued to look at me. I kept taking a few steps and then would look back and salute him. Each time I did, I found him still gazing at me. So we continued until I was out of sight.

"They all talked of Swami Turiyananda as being so stern. But in all my years of association with him, I saw him only as loving. Such affection and such love as we saw in these disciples of Sri Ramakrishna I have not seen anywhere else."

When Swami Prabhavananda returned to Calcutta from Banaras, he stayed with Boshi Sen for two months. During this time he had the opportunity to have the holy association of Swami Saradananda, who was nearby at the Udbodhan in Baghbazar. Swami remembered:

"Swami Saradananda was giving a class on the Vedanta Sutras with Shankara's commentary. I used to attend it every evening. Once he got mad at the reader and asked me, 'Can you read?' I was nervous, but I said, 'I can try.' I read something, and he said, 'You will do.' And so I became the reader. Then I began to realize what an opportunity I had missed in not having had more association with him. He was so sweet. He had always looked so stern and serious that I used to bow down to him quickly and run away.

"Once we asked Swami Saradananda, 'If a person has the four qualifications of a spiritual aspirant, is he not already illumined?' Swami Saradananda answered, 'Yes, that is true, but as you struggle you will attain illumination.'" The reference is to the four qualifications for spiritual attainment enumerated in Shankara's *Crest-Jewel of Discrimination*, namely discrimination, renunciation, the six treasures of virtue, and longing for liberation.

While staying at Boshi Sen's, Swami Prabhavananda began to make arrangements for his trip to Singapore. He told us, "One day I came out of the house and met Khoka Maharaj. He asked me, 'Where are you going?'

"'I am going to make reservations for Singapore.'

"'You are not going to Singapore. Go and see Swami Saradananda before you do anything else!'

"Swami Saradananda lived only one block away. I went to see him and told him what Khoka Maharaj had said to me. Then Swami Saradananda told me, 'We have other plans for you. You don't have to go to Singapore.' He asked me to go to Belur Math.

"The trustees of the math were meeting; Swamis Shivananda, Saradananda, Subodhananda, and Shuddhananda were there. I was ushered into the meeting. Swami Shivananda, the president, said, 'We have decided to send you to America. Will you go?'

"I answered, 'Of course, Maharaj, whatever you ask me to do I will do.'

"Then Swami Saradananda made the remark, 'Oh, he is so young!' There was a pindrop silence. He stared at me for a long time—maybe for five minutes. Then he said, 'He will do.' At that time I was twenty-nine and looked like a lad of nineteen.

"After the meeting I went back to Calcutta with Swami Saradananda in the same boat. Then we went to the Udbodhan; I was walking behind him. Right at the door of the Udbodhan, he turned to me and said, quoting a Bengali saying, 'So you are going to cross seven oceans and thirteen rivers.'

"'Yes, Maharaj,' I answered, 'you are sending me. But I feel nervous. What do I know that I can teach or preach?'

"Swami Saradananda replied in English, and his words are still ringing in my ears, 'That is none of your business! We shall see to that!' And they have seen to it!"

In 1923, the year Swami Prabhavananda came to America, his brother Amulya and several brothers' wives received initiation from Swami Shivananda. Gokul, Swami's younger brother, received initiation from Holy Mother. His youngest brother, Arabinda, received initiation from Swami Saradananda.*

When Swami Prabhavananda's mother met Mahapurush Maharaj, she too wanted to be initiated by him although she and her husband, Kumud, already had a family guru, a brahmin priest, as was the custom in those days. Mahapurush Maharaj said that she did not need to be initiated again. Jnanada once met Holy Mother in Vishnupur and later said that Holy Mother was very kind to her, called her "Abani's mother," and took great care of her.

Swami also had three sisters: Kiran, Lavanya, and Sushama. Lavanya became a disciple of Mahapurush Maharaj, as did Swami's nephew Asit.

Early in 1923, Swami Prabhavananda was present at the sannyas ceremony at Belur Math when Gurudas Maharaj, Swami's companion on the pilgrimage to Kedar-Badri, received his final vows. Swami said that Gurudas Maharaj had received initiation from Holy Mother. Gurudas' brahmacharya and sannyas guru was Swami Abhedananda. Gurudas Maharaj received the sannyas name of Atulananda.

Before Swami left India, Mahapurush Maharaj wanted him to get used to being in the presence of women, which was essential for a teacher in the West. So Mahapurush Maharaj sent Swami to teach at the Gadadhar Ashrama near Kalighat, in Calcutta. Swami related: "Many educated women from aristocratic families would come to the ashrama to study the Gita and Upanishads with me and to ask questions about the scriptures. Batches of women of different ages came all day long. I hardly had any privacy."

Swami also told us that around this time an incident took place through which Mahapurush Maharaj trained Swami for his future work: "This incident happened just before I came to America. A young boy prostrated before Mahapurush Maharaj. I was present. Mahapurush Maharaj accepted his obeisance as if a stranger had bowed down to him. The boy's feelings were

---

* Amulya and Arabinda were lawyers, like their father and maternal grandfather; Gokul was a school principal.

hurt, and he said, 'Maharaj, don't you remember me? I am your disciple. You showered your grace on me.' Mahapurush Maharaj replied, 'I don't know all that. Whoever comes to me, I throw at the feet of the Lord and let the Lord take care of him.' I had the feeling that Mahapurush Maharaj said this for my benefit, because I had to go away and teach. He did not think of himself as the guru. What humility he had!"

Swami shared with us several brief reminiscences concerning Mahapurush Maharaj. Swami gave the source only for the first of these, which was told him by Swami Gangeshananda, who had heard the story directly from Mahapurush Maharaj himself: "One day Mahapurush Maharaj wanted to know the Christ mantra. He had experienced a vision, and so it was related to him in English, 'Lord, have mercy on me.'

"A woman disciple of Mahapurush Maharaj came to him grief-stricken because her son had died. She asked the swami if he would do something so that she could see him. Mahapurush Maharaj said, 'All right, I will pray.' He began to think of the Lord, and the woman disciple saw her son with Thakur.

"Mahapurush Maharaj said at one time, 'A Ramakrishna loka [spiritual realm] has been created.'

"Lord Ronaldshay once visited Belur Math and mentioned in the course of conversation that Swami Vivekananda had founded the Ramakrishna Order. Mahapurush Maharaj corrected him, 'Oh, no, Sri Ramakrishna founded the order!'

"Mahapurush Maharaj used to see Sri Ramakrishna [in vision] every morning when he went to meditate, and Sri Ramakrishna would kiss him in the Indian way" [putting the fingers to the chin and then to his lips]."

Shortly before Swami Prabhavananda left for America, he went to pay his respects to M. [Mahendranath Gupta], the compiler of The Gospel of Sri Ramakrishna. Swami said to M. on this occasion, "'Sir, may I ask a boon of you?'

"'What is it?'

"'Would you please meditate on Thakur?'

"M. replied, 'Why, that is a wonderful boon!'"

While M. was seated with eyes closed, Swami bent down and

took the dust of M.'s feet. M., who never allowed any monk, no matter how junior, to make pranam to him, opened his eyes and said affectionately, "You rascal, you tricked me!" Then M. added, "You are going to the West. Shake hands with me!" And so they shook hands.

In April 1923, Swami Prabhavananda left India, accompanying Swami Prakashananda, who had received initiation from Holy Mother. Their ship stopped in Colombo, the capital of Ceylon,* before continuing the two-month journey to the United States of America.

---

* Currently, Sri Lanka.

CHAPTER FIVE

First Years in America

SWAMI PRABHAVANANDA FREQUENTLY told us what happened to him after he and Swami Prakashananda landed in Boston the first week of June 1923: "Originally I had been intended for Los Angeles. Swami Prakashananda had been given a thousand dollars by a woman, a disciple of Swami Sachchidananda (II), to bring a swami for the center there. The Los Angeles center had been started by Swami Sachchidananda, but he had gone back to India. Only when Swami Prakashananda and I arrived in Boston did we learn that Swami Paramananda had bought a place near Los Angeles [Ananda Ashrama]. Paramananda said he would take me as his assistant. I asked Swami Prakashananda what he wanted me to do. He said, 'You come with me to San Francisco.'"

Swami Prakashananda had been working in America since 1906, when Swami Trigunatitananda brought him to San Francisco as his assistant. In 1916, one year after Swami Trigunatitananda died, Swami Prakashananda became the head of the San Francisco center; and in 1923 Swami Prabhavananda became his assistant.

In later years, when we asked Swami Prabhavananda about his early experiences of lecturing, he said that his first lecture was in Colombo, on his way to America. He spoke there only for five or ten minutes. His second lecture was at the Vedanta Society of New York, where he spoke on Sri Ramakrishna. Once he was settled in Northern California, Swami Prakashananda slowly introduced his assistant to the routine of public speaking. Swami Prabhavananda related: "After I was in San Francisco for six months, Swami Prakashananda let me give a class on the Gita. That was easy. After a year, I gave Sunday lectures. The second Sunday I had prepared, but everything went blank. I was so nervous! I just said, 'That's all for tonight,' and walked out. After ten minutes Swami Prakashananda came and saw the temple empty. He came to my room and consoled me. Then he asked me, 'Why didn't you ask for questions?'

"At first I used to write out the whole lecture; later I just took notes. I got used to lecturing after I came to Portland [in 1925]."

Swami Prabhavananda's first impressions of life in the West were recorded in four letters that he wrote from San Francisco to Swami Siddheswarananda at the Madras math.

Swami Siddheswarananda had been a teacher before he became a disciple of Maharaj and joined the Ramakrishna Order. In a letter to his father, Ravi Varma, third prince of Cochin, Swami Siddheswarananda acknowledged Swami Prabhavananda's early influence on him: "I hope you have preserved the letter S. Prabhavananda, then Br. Bhakti Chaitanya, wrote to me while I was a teacher, inspiring me with the ideal of renunciation. You know he has helped me much in taking to this life, for which I shall be eternally grateful to him."

In this same letter, dated October 15, 1924, Swami Siddheswarananda wrote:

I am sending you some of the interesting letters written to me by S. Prabhavananda from America. Please do not forget to return them to me as I shall have to show them to some friends here. As he is the first Swami with whom you came in contact, you may be glad to know about his movements.

I had sent him some of the pickled chilies you sent us last year. He must have enjoyed them with Sushil Maharaj, S. Prakashananda.

Swami Prabhavananda's four letters are included here almost in their entirety. They give us a glimpse of a largely undocumented period in the American Vedanta work, decades before

Indian spirituality and culture became widely known and accepted. Moreover, the letters convey Swami Prabhavananda's feelings for his monastic brothers and friends and give an insight into his continuing interest in all matters concerning the Ramakrishna Math and Mission in India. As he was a Bengali and Swami Siddheswarananda a South Indian, they communicated in English.

The Hindu Temple
2963 Webster Street
San Francisco,
27th Feb., 1924

My dear brother,

Your very affectionate letter to hand. I am sorry I cannot write to you often though I wish I could. The reason is I find very little time to write letters, and so many I get from India (and you can imagine they all want long descriptive letters in reply) that it becomes almost impossible to reply to all in due time. I hope you will excuse me, as you can imagine my situation. Then again I have to prepare myself for two lectures every week. Well, you write that you have been disappointed as I did not send you any lecture. It is not an easy job as you think. I do not write out my lectures. I note down points, and elaborate them in my mind and then go to the platform and finish with the job. And I become too idle to write it out again after the lecture has been delivered. There is no shorthand reporter, as none amongst our students knows to take down in shorthand. But we expect shortly to get one, as one student is just learning with a view to take down our lectures. Anyway, I am just sending you the lecture I gave last Sunday. Hope you will forgive me.

You want some personal touches in my letters and not simple business letters. Well, volumes can be written what interesting things happen every week. And so it is better to remain silent. Is it not? One incident I am writing to you as long as you are so eager to know. The other day in the Gita class I spoke about Incarnate Teachers and Incarnations while explaining the text of the Gita. When I invited questions, a lady asked me, "Swami, don't you think there is a universal wish for God to incarnate again?" What to reply? I said, "Madam, I do not know of the *universal wish*. But I can speak of *my wish*: I know for certain God has incarnated Himself already in this age, and His work is just begun. I do not see any reason for your so-called universal wish. Then suppose God comes down and talks to you as a man, would you accept Him? No, unless you are ready. How many did accept Jesus in his lifetime?" When she again asked who is the Incarnation in the present age, I had to take the name of the Master [Sri Ramakrishna]. Well, you know we do not preach the personality of the Master, and there were many who were quite surprised at my boldness, though they liked it.

The other day we had a hundred miles' ride in an automobile in one day. We started at half past nine in the morning and came back at midnight. We enjoyed the trip very much.

By the time this letter reaches you, I hope you have become a Swami, and you have always the blessings of Maharaj and Guru Maharaj [Sri Ramakrishna].

I am glad to learn everything about Divyananda and glad to learn that he remembers me kindly. I had asked you to send him some best cigarettes when he was in Bangalore and charge the price to our account here. You did not write anything about it. Did you send him the cigarettes? You know, if a drunkard is not in good humour, give a drink and he will be all right. So if Divyananda is not in good humour, bribe him with cigarettes! Yes, that is the secret. And Rishi Babu—does he remember me? I am sending him something in a separate cover, but please don't tell him that I sent it. That will humour him. [As disclosed in a later letter, this "something" was a Valentine card.]

I am expecting the reply to my letter to Swamiar. I have not received it as yet. Please give him my Sashtangam [most respectful pranam].

I am sending a photograph that was taken some time back, but we received it only the other day. You will find there how we dress at home. We are standing in front of the sunroom—a little cabin with glass walls.

We are having fine weather now. It is cool and pleasant. It does not snow here in winter as in New York. Temperature there sometimes comes down to some points below 0 degree.

S. Paramananda is now in the ashrama near Los Angeles and is doing well. A student of his is conducting the work in Boston.

Sushil Maharaj is doing well and he sends you his love and blessings. Please accept my love and best wishes and remember me to all the brothers of the monastery and friends in Madras.

Hope you are all keeping good health. Give my love to Krishnan. Who is looking after the garden in Madras? Is the bower still there? Any new plants planted? Do you get enough flowers for worship?

Now I write something about business: As soon as I received your letter, I handed over the second volume of *The Great Master* [*Sri Ramakrishna: The Great Master,* by Swami Saradananda] to a friend requesting him to edit carefully. He is an old man staying in our temple. Brahmachari Atmaram is his name, and he is a student of Trigunatita, a well-read man. He stays in our Temple for eight months in a year as a Tapasvi [religious ascetic] and then goes out and works for four months, earns enough money to sustain himself for the rest of the year.

Please tell Ramu that I have asked the Parry Pictures Company of Boston to send him a catalogue of pictures. They have all the best pictures of the world of the greatest artists. But they are of a small size. They are very cheap. Please tell him that I would like him to select some pictures for the school children as they have a great educative value. They can be hung on the walls of the classrooms not for decoration only but for teaching history, geography, and even natural science. Please let me know the pictures

he wants, and I will send the order from here.
With my love and best wishes to you all,
Yours affly,
Prabhavananda

Vedanta Society of San Francisco
2963 Webster Street, San Francisco
25th April 1924

My dear brother,

Your affectionate card. I am so glad to learn that you have taken the holy vow of sannyas. "Kulam pavitram janani krtartha" [the family is purified; the mother is blessed]. I wish and pray from the deepest core of my heart that Sri Sri Guru Maharaj may make your life blessed to yourself and many that come in contact with you.

Well, what makes you think that I withdraw myself in matters of correspondence? Don't I reply to every letter that I get from you? It may be sometimes I am late in replying. But as I explained in some other letter, my time is not my own here. Considering my situation, I hope you will excuse me if sometimes I delay in replying to the letters. Anyway, brother, your love and affection for me will never allow me to withdraw myself from you.

As usual, I am giving one public lecture every week and holding the Gita class. The attendance is regular. When we announce a catchy subject, the hall gets crowded. Week before last I spoke on the "science of breathing." Great many new people came to hear me. After the lecture they all wanted to learn breathing exercises. I referred them to Swami Prakasanandaji. When they were told about *Yama* [ethical practices] and *Niyama*, [observances of virtues], they were scared. Funny world, isn't it?

Young girls with "red ink" on their lips and their faces painted come to learn about Vedanta philosophy, if the philosophy can make them succeed in their love affairs. This is the *world*, brother. What our people in India do privately within the bolted doors, the people here do that publicly and speak to all about it.

Last Sunday was Easter Day and I spoke on Renunciation, a summary of which I am sending for the *Kesari*. The second volume of *The Great Master* has been edited, and I am sending you the book.

I am sorry to learn that Rishiji is suffering from rheumatism. Well, everyone has to pay taxes to the body, as the Master used to say.

I had informed you that S. Prakasananda had undergone an operation in his eye sometime back. The second operation will be done in May. And he will have to remain in the hospital for a fortnight. In June he will go to Shanti Ashrama with some students for the summer Yoga classes, and I will have to remain here during his absence and hold the classes and continue the Sunday lectures as usual. Oh! I am already getting tired of speaking. Week after week to speak on religion to the same audience — what a task!

The other day I received a letter from Miss MacLeod and was glad to learn that Dr. Demello is his old self again. I hear he is helping the old lady in her anti-malarial campaign.

You will be interested to know the names of eatables they advertise here in the restaurants. I am sure the very names will draw water from your mouths. They are "Hot dogs," "Hush puppies," "Fat Boy Barbecue," "Fat Girl Sandwiches." Can you imagine that? *Vive la* your *Rasam! Karambu!*

I sent some pictures to Ramu. I have not received any news if he has received them. I am so glad to learn that the "Students' Home" has grown so wonderfully. The Vidyapith at Deoghar is now on a stable basis, we learn. How is the work of Matri Mandir at Madras progressing?

Will you kindly send some six copies of *Vedanta Kesari*, which contains the article of Durga Devi, to the address of Mrs. Clara M. Pettee, Hindu Temple. She asked me to write you for the same, but I forgot. So please try to send as early as possible.

How is Swamiar? Why don't I get any reply to my letter? How is the work in Bombay progressing? Is Suresh M. of Mayavati [Swami Yatiswarananda] going to take charge of the Bombay centre? What about the centre at Ahmedabad and Mysore? Is Jiten Maharaj still in Madras? Where is Divyananda? Has he gone to Bombay? How are all friends in Madras? Please remember me to all and give them my best regards.

We are well. Hope this finds you in good health.

Please accept our love and best wishes,

Yours affly,

Prabhavananda

The Hindu Temple
San Francisco, Calif. U.S.A.
6th June 1924

My dear brother,

Your affectionate note with all the interesting information made me so happy. My thanks for the same.

Swami Prakasanandaji had undergone the second operation on the 29th of May last. He is still in the hospital and doing well. He may have to stay there for another week.

Before the operation was done we both went to the Shanti Ashrama and stayed for about ten days. We had a lively time up there. It is so [words missing] and solitary like our ashramas in the Himalayas. And the spiritual atmosphere! One could feel it tangibly. The spirit of Hari Maharaj [Swami Turiyananda] is still vibrating. Hari Maharaj once said that the atmosphere of spirituality that he created there would remain for at least a century. Oh, it was such a relief, you can imagine, after a stay in a crowded, luxurious city.

A friend drove us in her machine and we enjoyed the ride up hills amidst gorgeous scenery. She also brought us back and while coming back met with a little accident. As our machine was turning round a corner on the hill, another car from the opposite side came and dashed against ours. Our chauffeur was an expert driver, and she stopped the machine immediately. There was no substantial damage done to our car, only a front light was broken. But the other car (a Ford) was smashed, though no person met with any injury. Then of course we drove back happily and safely home.

Some pictures were taken at the ashrama which I am sending you.

Our classes here remain closed in the month of … I am giving one lecture on Sunday mornings. After Swami Prakasanandaji gets better, and when he is able to resume his work, I may be going to stay with Swami Paramananda at his ashrama at La Crescenta for some time. But I don't know if they can accommodate me as I was told they have not enough accommodation. Anyway, I have written to stay there; got no reply as yet.

A friend took notes of some of my lectures. He will give them to me shortly. After I get them, I will edit and send one or two for the *V.K.*

I am so glad to learn that Panditji, Mahadevan and Damodar got sannyas this time. You did not write to me about Yogesh M. Where is he now, and how is he doing?

I am glad Rishiji appreciated the Valentine cards I sent him. There is a lover's day, or the Valentine Day, as it is called here, in a year, and on that day they send cards with all sorts of funny writings. A friend brought me some for fun and I sent them to Rishiji.

Swami Suddhanandaji wrote me a letter asking Swami Prakasananda to come back to India as, he wrote, we need a leader in India who has come in touch with Western ideas. I wrote him back to say that it was impossible to spare Swami Prakasanandaji from America. But I gave him a suggestion. I asked one of the senior Swamis [possibly Swamis Shuddhananda, Shankarananda, or Sharvananda] to come and stay in this country for a year or two and then go back to India and work. I have especially requested Sudhir M. [Swami Shuddhananda] to come here and in that case, I wrote, I could go out to beg his passage money. He won't have to work but will stay as the Mahant [abbot]. Don't you think that a very happy suggestion?

Please remember me to all the friends in Madras and give them my love and best wishes.

Convey my Sashtangam to Mahapurushji and Swami Shar-
vanandaji and accept yourself my love and best wishes.
Yours affly,
Prabhavananda

P.S. I shall let you know what I can do for editing the *Gospel*
[*The Gospel of Sri Ramakrishna*] through some friend.

The Hindu Temple
San Francisco, Calif., U.S.A. Sept. 5, 1924

My dear brother,

Your affectionate letter. I am sending you the lecture of Swamiji on "Women of India" already published. You can repro-
duce the lecture in the *Vedanta Kesari* with the Introduction
which I am separately sending along with a lecture of Swami
Prakasanandaji and one of mine. You will have ample food
for the magazine. You can publish the lecture on "Women of
India" in a pamphlet form as we have done here and sell it in
India. As the cost of printing, etc. is very high, it is not advisa-
ble to sell the book published from here in India. So, we give
the Madras Centre the right of publication, of course, unconditionally. We give the right to the *P.B.* [*Prabuddha Bharata*] to
incorporate in the *Complete Works*. I am also sending you the
three pamphlets of Swami Prakasananda. I had talks with
him, and he wants you to publish those lectures from India.
He gives you the right of publication unconditionally.

You have asked for some good American magazines for
exchange. But that is impossible in this country. Anyway, I
shall try to send you some magazines occasionally.

A few days back I went to pay a visit to the ashrama at La
Crescenta. It is a wonderful place. Had a very pleasant time
there. Stayed for about 10 days. I will soon write to you a
short account of my visit there for publication in the *Kesari*,
as Swami Paramananda wanted me to write about it for any
of the magazines in India. I went there for a rest, but there
also the sisters teased me to give lectures. As a last resort I
told Swami Paramananda not to ask me as I wanted a little

good time and not bother about lectures. So I was relieved of the task. But the day I was to leave, Swami gave a farewell party and invited many friends for dinner. We were having chats at the table when suddenly a sister got up and introduced me formally to the party and requested me to speak something. It was an embarrassing situation. I looked at my watch and said that there was not time enough to enable me to make a long speech. But I spoke for a short while and thanked them all for their brotherly feeling towards me. Then there began jokes and fun at the table. Everyone said some funny story. Then came my turn. One of the menfolks who told the funniest story, I wanted him to point his finger to his head and asked him what was the abbreviation for mountain? He had to reply, pointing to his head "mt" (empty). There was a roar of laughter. S. Paramananda said, "You can't beat the Hindus."

Swami went away to Boston for a month. They all wanted me to stay there for some more days. But I could not, as S. Prakasananda wanted me back soon.

Well, you wanted to know the routine of our life here. Just to give you a rough idea: I get up early in the morning; have my bath and then sit for meditation in my room for an hour or so. Then prepare the breakfast. We have to do our own cooking. In the meanwhile, S. Prakasananda gets up and finishes his bath. We take our breakfast at 8:30. After breakfast we have to do the washing up of the dishes. So practically I am free after 9:30. Then attend to letters and enquiries till 11 a.m. At 11 some friends come for meditation. We meditate together for half an hour. S. Prakasananda gives interviews to students in the morning. At 12 noon, I go out for a walk. Come back at 2. Take some fruits and a glass of milk. Then make a little study till 4. At 4:30 go out marketing. Begin cooking and we have our dinner before 7 in the evening. The menu consists of dhal, bhat, chachahari curry, sometimes fish or meat. Two nights in a week I am tied up for lectures. At other nights, friends come for dinner, or we go to dinner at friends' houses occasionally and chat with them. When we have no friends, we hear the

radio or go to the moving pictures. Once a week, we go mo-
toring out of the city and have our dinner in some restau-
rant. Retire to bed at ten in the evening. Thus, you see, we
have practically little time left at our own disposal. This is
just to give you a rough idea how we live here.

I am sending you one copy of "Women of India" for Mahapurushji Maharaj and another for Tejnarayan Maharaj [Swami
Sharvananda]. Please hand them over to them.

Yes, we read the *Kesari* with interest, and I congratulate
you for ably conducting it.

Glad to learn that Panditji [*identity uncertain*] has gone to
take charge of the work in Ceylon. Is Suresh Maharaj going
to take charge of the work in Bombay?

We hear that Amulya Maharaj [Swami Shankarananda] is
coming to this country for a visit. Just the rumour we hear.
He has not written anything. It will be nice if he comes here,
and we wish he would stay in this country. I asked S. Paramananda if he would like to have more Swamis to help him
in his work. He replied that he is seriously thinking of going
to India next year and bringing two Swamis with him. Well,
I don't know if he would be able to go back to India next
year, for the plan of work at his ashrama will take several
more years to be accomplished. And he won't go before he
has carried out his plans.

We are doing well. Trust this finds you all in good health.
Please give my Sashtangams to Sri Sri Mahapurushji Maharaj
and Swamiar and accept yourself my love and best wishes.

Please remember me to all the brothers of the Math ... and
give them all my love and best wishes.
Yours affly,
Prabhavananda

After Swami Prabhavananda was in San Francisco for two
years, his lectures and classes were attracting a larger attendance than those of the senior swami. He thought of ending this
embarrassing situation by suggesting to Swami Prakashananda one day, "Don't you think we should spread out?" Swami

Prabhavananda related: "Swami Prakashananda was so affectionate with me. He was just like an older brother. He said yes, but he asked Mrs. Pettee to go with me. I had to take her."

And so Swami Prabhavananda went to Portland in September or October 1925. He recalled: "I went to Portland with $40 and train fare, and spent $40 for advertising and renting a lecture hall. After ten days' lecturing, I got back $40. That is how I started the Portland work."

In Portland, the young Prabhavananda was known as the "Militant Swami." Whenever the crowd dropped off, he would talk on reincarnation. Once he announced the topic "On Becoming Rich through Psychology." A large crowd came. Swami scolded his audience, "You have come to hear *me*, who have no bank account, lecture to you on how to get rich through psychology. Aren't you fools!" Then, Swami said, he spoke on Christ, who did not know where to lay his head.

Establishing the Vedanta work in the 1920s and 1930s in America was an uphill task. Many people still associated "yoga" and "swamis" with acquiring wealth, beauty, and psychic powers. Occasionally the swamis encountered racial prejudice. And during the Depression it was difficult for the small number of devotees to give the new Vedanta centers the needed financial support.

Swami Prabhavananda admitted: "I did not always have complete faith when I came to this country. When I was in Portland during the Depression, they did not know how the work could be continued. One day I stood by Swamiji's painting and asked him, 'Do you want me to go back?' The next day I got a letter from Sister [Lalita] that she wanted to come to Portland."

"Sister" was Mrs. Carrie Mead Wyckoff, who with her sisters Helen Mead and Shanti [Mrs. Alice Mead Hansbrough] had lived in a rented home in South Pasadena at the turn of the century. Shanti was a disciple of Swami Vivekananda, and Swamiji had stayed at the sisters' home at 309 Monterey Road for six weeks during the winter of 1899–1900.

In July 1900, Swami Turiyananda spent a few days as the Mead sisters' guest in South Pasadena. During his two-week stay in Southern California, they took him to see the famous orange groves and the ocean. Sometime between 1900 and 1902, Carrie became Swami Turiyananda's disciple. One day he told her, "You will have work to do, but it will be quiet work."

Carrie also met Swami Trigunatitananda, who gave her the name of Lalita. In later years, Carrie was usually called Sister Lalita or Sister. In 1928, almost thirty years after Swami Turiyananda's prediction of Sister's future work, Swami Prabhavananda went from Portland to Los Angeles to give a series of lectures. Swami Prabhavananda told us: "A woman from Alhambra, whom I had met in San Francisco, had come to Portland. She invited me to go to Los Angeles to give three lectures. She rented the Music Hall where Swamiji had spoken. Sister and Shanti came to a lecture and met me. Before I left Los Angeles to return to Portland, they asked me if they could join me in Portland. We wanted to build an ashrama there. Sister bought land near Lake Oswego, but the Christian Scientists objected. When we got her down payment of $1,000 back, I felt relieved. Then Sister told me about her house in Hollywood. I wrote to Mahapurush Maharaj, and he wrote back, 'Yes, I give you permission to open a center in Los Angeles.' But I had to wait for Vividishananda to come to Portland."

Finally, in December 1929, Swami Prabhavananda was able to accept Sister Lalita's invitation and moved into her home in Hollywood, which her brother, William Mead, had given her. The house was located at 1946 Ivar Avenue, later renamed Vedanta Place.

A few years before Swami came to Hollywood, Sister had lost a son just about Swami's age, and throughout their relationship she regarded Swami both as a son and as a guru. He often said, "Sister and I lived together for more than twenty years, and there was never a harsh word between us."

The beginnings of Swami Prabhavananda's public work in Los Angeles were not greeted with unanimous enthusiasm. Swami told us: "As soon as I arrived in Los Angeles, Swami Paramananda opened a center on Adams Street. Devamata wrote to Mahapurush Maharaj that I must not be allowed there. Mahapurush Maharaj wrote me that he gave her the answer, 'Paramananda does not own the city of Los Angeles.' The disciples of Thakur were so affectionate. We were like their nephews. Anything we asked, they let us do. They had the vision."

At first, Swami spoke in a lecture hall at the Garden Apartments on Sycamore and Hollywood Boulevard. Swami told us, "Rent for the hall was $7.50, and the collection would be $10." Later he lectured at the Music Center, near Tenth Street, because it was more centrally located. Sometime in 1930, in order to discourage seekers of eternal youth and metaphysical shoppers, he stopped advertising and began holding meetings in the living room of Sister's house. That was the beginning of the Vedanta Society of Southern California.

According to Amiya, the Englishwoman who stayed in Sister's home from the early 1930s onward for almost twenty years, two rooms were added in 1933 by dint of stringent economy and with the help of various donations. The smaller of the rooms was dedicated as a shrine room, and the sacred relics were installed in it.

Swami Prabhavananda told us that a short form of the ritual worship was done daily before the Hollywood temple was built. It was begun the year Swami Nikhilananda came to America, bringing the relics for Hollywood. These were the relics Mahapurush Maharaj gave to Swami Nikhilananda as he was leaving for the United States to become Swami Akhilananda's assistant. Mahapurush Maharaj gave Swami Nikhilananda the relics on the condition that he would divide them with Swami Prabhavananda.

Asked when he began to initiate, Swami Prabhavananda told us that he started in Hollywood in 1931. "After one or two years in Hollywood, I felt I had to begin. When it came to what mantra to give, Maharaj helped me. Before Vijayananda left India, Mahapurush Maharaj told him what mantras to give initiates. When Vijayananda came to America, he told me what Mahapurush Maharaj had said to him and confirmed what I was giving."

Swami Prabhavananda occasionally spoke of the financial problems he and the young Vedanta centers encountered during the

Depression years, and how the Lord provided: "In Portland I had a very hard time. And I had a hard time here in Hollywood. I don't think any other swami in this country went through the hardship I went through. We lacked for food. We couldn't afford cream for our coffee. For supper we had popcorn and milk for some time. No one knew our situation. When we had a $10 collection, we thought we were doing well.

"A colored maid by the name of Ruby supported us for about six months. She brought food and cooked for us." Swami said that after the six months were over, Ruby vanished; they never saw her again.

"We didn't have money to pay taxes. [X] had an interview with me and put money in my hand. I didn't count it and put it in my pocket. Vireswar [Biarney Folling] was the treasurer then. He told me, 'Swami, we have to pay taxes.' I took the bills out of my pocket: $20, $20, $20—$500!

"Another time we had to pay taxes on a Monday. We owed $150. On Sunday, Aparna [Elizabeth Tierney]—we didn't know her very well then—put a $50 check in the collection basket. Monday morning I picked up Tantine [Josephine MacLeod] at the railway station in Glendale. The first thing she said when she came to the center was, 'Give me a pen!' She wrote a check for $100."

Twelve years after Swami Prabhavananda's arrival in America, friends provided him with funds to take a much-needed rest and go to India. Accompanied by Sister Lalita, he left on a pilgrimage to India in August 1935.

CHAPTER SIX

Pilgrimage in 1935

On the way to India, Swami Prabhavananda and Sister Lalita stopped in Japan. Swami enjoyed the sights, and in a letter dated August 13, 1935, he wrote to his disciple Aparna [Elizabeth Tierney]:

> Yesterday at one o'clock in the afternoon we got down at Yokohama ... At Kamakura we saw the large bronze statue of Buddha. The statue is simply huge, placed in the open air. Two hillocks form the background and the garden is beautiful. We went inside the statue of Buddha and felt that the Lord is the body of the universe, and we are entering His body. Inside the statue, there is another shrine of Buddha, which is inspiring. We visited two more temples at Kamakura and then took the train for Tokyo. And here we are. We went out for a walk and visited the N.Y.K. office. Then had a glimpse of His Imperial Majesty who arrived in Tokyo today.
>
> We have had a very pleasant voyage so far. And at every step we feel the protection and care of the Lord.

—————

During his travels in India, Swami Prabhavananda had the privilege of associating with two direct disciples of Sri Ramakrishna, Swamis Akhandananda and Vijnanananda. Swami Akhandananda was then the president of the Ramakrishna Math and Mission. Swami Prabhavananda told us: "I went to visit Swami Akhandananda in his ashrama at Sargachi. After I entered the gate, I passed through a long road to meet him in the house when suddenly firecrackers went off on both sides of the road. I found Swami Akhandananda seated on a chair, and there was an empty chair by his side. I prostrated before him and asked, 'Maharaj, what is all this business of firecrackers?' He answered, 'Why, my nephew comes after so many years to visit me from such a long distance as America! Should I not welcome him?' Then he held my hand and wanted me to sit on the empty chair, thinking perhaps that after so many years in America I was not used to sitting on the floor any more. But I objected, saying, 'This is my place, Maharaj.' Then I sat down at his feet and began to massage them.

"Once I asked him if he would come to America. And like a little boy, he became excited and said, yes, he would come with me if I would take him. I was making preparations for it when the trustees and other swamis intervened and would not let him come.

"One evening, when I went to his room at Belur Math, I saw how he was troubled with mosquitoes. He had covered himself with a chaddar. I said, 'I have something with me. I'll rub a little on your feet, and then the mosquitoes will not bother you.' So I rubbed a little citronella on his feet. He pleased me by saying, 'What magic you know!'

"One day Swami Akhandananda wanted to play cards, just like a little boy. I did not want to play; I wanted to hear him talk, but I could not refuse him. So I made a deal with Swami Gangesananda, who was our opponent, that as soon as the game began he would cheat, and I would catch him red-handed. And so it was done. I said, 'Maharaj, look how he is cheating!' Swami Akhandananda got excited and threw away his cards. And then he began to talk to us about his travels in Tibet.

"Once he was traveling in the Himalayas; he lost his way. He was on the peak of a mountain and did not know which way to go. He slid and fell down into a field. A man saw him and took him into his home. That man said that nobody had ever come back alive from that mountain, which was infested by wild animals.

"Swami Akhandananda spoke so dramatically and fluently— charming. It was a joy to hear him talk."

Swami Prabhavananda used to relate a couple of other incidents concerning Swami Akhandananda:

"A devotee used to take Swami Akhandananda to meet some important people, but Swami Akhandananda would never speak on spiritual matters—always on other things. This disappointed the devotee. One day he said to Swami Akhandananda, 'Sir, why do you keep yourself hidden like this?' Swami Akhandananda replied, 'Publicity is no good.'

"At one time Swami Akhandananda was the guest of a rich devotee. The Swami kept writing to Swamiji for a long time how generous, kind, and compassionate this devotee was. Then he stopped writing about him. Swamiji wrote back, 'What happened to your good man?' Swami Akhandananda answered, 'Oh, Swamiji, I am so disillusioned. He has a mistress.' Swamiji wrote to him, 'Do you expect everybody to be a Sukadeva [perfected soul] like you?'"

———

Swami Prabhavananda's association with Swami Vijnanananda during this pilgrimage came about in an interesting way. Swami Prabhavananda often related the circumstances:

"When I returned to India after twelve years in the USA, I had the good fortune of spending a few days in the blessed company of Swami Vijnanananda. At that time Vijnan Maharaj was the vice-president of the order. He came to Belur Math, and that morning I went to visit him. As I prostrated before him, he inquired, 'Who is this form of Narayana?' Though I was wearing gerua robes, I had long hair. Swami Omkarananda introduced me, saying that I had recently arrived from America and was a disciple of Sri Maharaj. I told Vijnan Maharaj that I hoped to see my aged mother in Vishnupur and wished to visit Jayrambati and Kamarpukur on the way. At once he said, 'I have never seen those places. Will you take me with you?'

"I replied, 'Certainly, Maharaj, it will be a great blessing for me.' But after a couple of hours, Vijnan Maharaj sent for me and said, 'I am sorry, Abani, I can't go. Bharat [Swami Abhayananda] says that many devotees from distant parts of India will be arriving at that time for initiation, and they would be disappointed.'

"But I told Bharat Maharaj before Swami Vijnanananda that there was an easy solution to this problem by fixing a later date for initiation and informing the devotees by telegram, for which I would bear the expenses. Having heard everything, Vijnan Maharaj remarked, pointing to me, 'He can solve problems so easily!'

"Before starting on our journey, I had requested my younger brother, who was headmaster of the school in Vishnupur, to make arrangements for a reception for Vijnan Maharaj. When we arrived at the railway station in Vishnupur, about three hundred schoolboys came to the station to receive us, and girls showered flowers on us.

"In Vishnupur, Swami Vijnanananda initiated several devotees in the shrine room of our ancestral home. Later my younger brother put a marble plaque there that Swami Vijnanananda, a direct disciple of Sri Ramakrishna, had given initation here. Swami Vijnanananda's picture is also there.

"My niece, a little girl about nine years old, went to her mother one day and said, 'Mother, won't you have from Maharaj what others are getting today?' My sister replied that she had already received the grace.

"'But Mother, can't I have it?'

"'No, you are too young.'

"I was listening to their conversation, amused. My niece turned to me and said, 'Please, Uncle, I want it from Maharaj.'

"I said, 'I'll see what I can do.' Then I went to Swami Vijnanananda in the shrine room and told him the situation. He said, 'Bring her here.' So she was also initiated that day.

"Arrangements were soon made for our visit to Jayrambati and Kamarpukur. One day, as Swami Vijnanananda was served dinner, my mother was standing near him. She said, 'Maharaj, I am coming with you to Jayrambati and Kamarpukur.'

"Vijnan Maharaj replied, 'We have no room in the car for you.' My mother insisted, 'Maharaj, you will have to take me with you.'

He answered, 'I am telling you there is no room. If you insist, then sit on my head and go!'

"At this point my mother wound the end of her cloth around her neck in a gesture of reverence, prostrated before him and said, 'Oh, no, you will give me room at your feet.' Then Swami Vijnanananda laughed and said, 'Well, you win.'

"We rented a car and a bus. Swami Vijnanananda, Sister Lalita, and I went in the car. My mother took the bus with some other family members and the swamis, brahmacharis, and devotees from the Bankura math, who had come for the occasion.

"Going to Kamarpukur and Jayrambati with a disciple of Sri Ramakrishna was a wonderful pilgrimage indeed. In both places, Swami Vijnanananda was absorbed in meditation, with eyes closed. In those days there was no accommodation for so many people to stay at Kamarpukur or Jayrambati, so we returned the same day to Vishnupur.

"After we returned to Vishnupur, Swami Vijnanananda remarked, 'Isn't Sister Lalita wonderful! We traveled in the same car for so many hours, and she never said a word. How quiet!' The American ladies with whom Vijnan Maharaj had had occasion to associate were lively, talkative types.

"One day Swami Maheshwarananda, the head of the Bankura math, came to Vishnupur and requested Vijnan Maharaj to visit Bankura since many devotees there were eager for initiation. But Swami Vijnanananda flatly refused to go. He told him, 'If Abani wants me to go, I will go.' After two or three days, Swami Maheshwarananda came to me and said, 'Brother, this is the situation. Please say a word on my behalf so that Vijnan Maharaj will come to Bankura.

"I was in a fix. I said, 'How can I ask him to go? We are not only enjoying his divine company, but he is a guest in our home.' But Swami Maheshwarananda insisted. Both of us went together and stood before Swami Vijnanananda with folded palms. Seeing this, he said to me, 'So you want me to go?'

"'No, Maharaj, it is not that; my only appeal is that you kindly give liberation to the devotees who are waiting for you at the Bankura monastery.' He left the next day for Bankura.

"I feel that I got this blessed opportunity to live in Swami Vijnanananda's holy company for about two weeks as a result of the long-standing wish of Maharaj that I should be under Vijnan Maharaj's protection."

Shortly after Swami Prabhavananda had received the vows of brahmacharya, Maharaj had thought of sending him to Swami Vijnanananda's monastery at Allahabad. He had told him, "You will be protected by the shade of a huge tree." Then Maharaj had said that Swami Vijnanananda was a hidden *brahmajnani* [knower of Brahman] and that after Swami Ramakrishnananda he was the greatest devotee of Sri Ramakrishna.

To illustrate this point, Maharaj told Swami Prabhavananda the following story:

"When I was in Allahabad with Vijnan, a young college student came to me and asked for spiritual instructions. I told him, 'I am a guest here. Go to Swami Vijnanananda, the abbot of this monastery.' But Vijnan sent the boy back to me. I asked him again to go to Vijnan, who alone could give spiritual instruction in this monastery. And the poor boy was sent back to me once more. When I made him go to Vijnan for a third time, the latter said, 'Alright, Maharaj wants me to teach you, so I will. Wait a minute!' He opened a trunk, took out a photograph of me, gave it to the boy, and said: 'Pray every day before this picture, and ask for guidance. If you do, you will attain your goal.'"

After relating this incident, Maharaj remarked to Swami Prabhavananda, "Do you see what a great devotee of Sri Ramakrishna Vijnan is?" Swami Prabhavananda used to tell us, "Maharaj had no sense of ego or existence separate from Sri Ramakrishna. In his own eyes as well as his brother disciples' eyes, he was completely identified with his master, and therefore any love for him was the same as love for Sri Ramakrishna."

Maharaj had later changed his mind, and instead of sending Swami Prabhavananda to Allahabad he decided to send him to Mayavati. But Swami Prabhavananda always felt that Maharaj's wish that he associate with Swami Vijnanananda was fulfilled in a wonderful manner during his pilgrimage in 1935.

One day, in Vishnupur, Swami Prabhavananda told Swami Vijnanananda what Maharaj had said about his devotion to Sri Ramakrishna. Swami Vijnanananda humbly replied, "Ah, Maharaj saw an ocean of goodness in a drop!"

Only on rare occasions did Swami Vijnanananda talk about his many spiritual visions. Once he told Swami Prabhavananda the following experience, which the latter noted in his diary the same day:

"'I went to visit Sarnath.* Suddenly I lost all physical consciousness; my mind seemed almost to have vanished. I was enveloped in an ocean of light, the light that is vibrant with peace, joy, and knowledge. I felt as if I were living in Buddha. I do not remember how long I remained in that state. The guide thought that I had fallen asleep, and as it was getting late, he tried to awaken me and so brought me back to normal consciousness. Later, when I went to visit the temple of Vishwanath in Banaras, I thought to myself, 'Why have I come here? To look at a stone?' when the same vision opened up. It was as if Vishwanath were telling me, 'The light is the same here as there—Truth is one.'"

Swami Vijnanananda told Swami Prabhavananda that one time after Sri Ramakrishna had locked the doors and windows of his room, he asked the monastic disciples to sit in a circle. And then he gave them a taste of the *Rasalila*—the divine play of Sri Krishna with the gopis, or cowherd girls.

During Swami Prabhavananda's pilgrimage in 1935, he wrote several more letters to Aparna, who carefully preserved them. Aparna was the principal of an elementary school in Hollywood and a member of the Vedanta Society of Southern California to the end of her life. The letters Swami wrote her from India are not only helpful in acquainting us with the chronology of his pilgrimage, but they constitute a valuable record of Swami's impressions and experiences.

In a letter to Aparna from Belur Math, dated November 28, 1935, Swami Prabhavananda wrote:

---

* The deer park in the city of Sarnath, near Banaras, is where Buddha preached his first sermon after illumination.

In my letter to Amiya I informed her of our visit to the birth-places of Holy Mother and Sri Ramakrishna. From Vishnu-pur we went to Bankura, where I delivered two lectures at the college hall. Then at the demand of the public I had to give another lecture in the open air. It is thrilling to see the enthusiasm of the public. Thousands came to hear. And I spoke in Bengali. The message of our master falls like gentle rain on thirsty soil. From Bankura we went to Khatra, a village. There they received us with a procession headed by the pictures of the Master and Swamiji and the crowd chanting and singing the name of the Lord. We stayed there for four days. Gave three lectures. People—men, women, children—would be crowding the place where we were living, and from three o'clock in the morning some would be waiting just to have a "glimpse." They would be shouting, "Victory to Sri Ramakrishna," "Victory to Divine Mother," "Victory to Swamiji."

Swami Prabhavananda gave a few more details about his lectures in Khatra in informal talks with his disciples. He said to us one day, "At Khatra I was lecturing in Bengali. Then I was asked to speak in English. My mother and all the women stayed during my English talk. Afterward I asked my mother, 'How come you stayed on? You don't understand English.' Then she said, 'But we wanted to hear your voice.'"

Swami said that during their stay in Bengal his mother became very fond of Sister Lalita, and Sister liked Jnanada very much. They had a good time laughing and talking, although Sister spoke only English and Jnanada Bengali.

During this trip Swami saw his mother for the last time. She told him about her worship of Sri Ramakrishna, "Thakur does not wait to go through the ritual when I offer him sweets; he takes the offering right from my hand."

Swami told us that during the last days of her life his mother always had a gerua cloth by her side. She thought that Swami Kashishwarananda, who was also a disciple of Maharaj, was her Abani. When she was on her deathbed someone brought a priest, as it is customary for the dying to receive absolution. Swami's mother objected, "Why should I atone? I have not committed any sin. And I have a son who is a monk."

Continuing his letter of November 28, 1935, to Aparna, Swami Prabhavananda wrote:

We came back to the Math [Belur] day before yesterday. In about a week the public of Calcutta will give us a reception, after which we leave for northern India on our pilgrimage.

Sister is standing the "thrills" very well. While she visited Holy Mother's and Sri Ramakrishna's birthplaces she remarked, "Am I dreaming or is it real?"

At times it seems to me also as if I am in a land of dreams. But again when I see the poverty of the land, my heart weeps for my people. Why should there be such conditions the Lord alone knows!

Swami's next letter to Aparna, dated January 17, 1936, was written from the Ramakrishna Mission Home of Service in Varanasi:

We visited Brindaban and Allahabad and came to Banaras. We expect to be here for three weeks. We enjoyed our visits at Brindaban and Allahabad. Brindaban is the birthplace of Sri Krishna. There He had His divine play with the gopis. I felt a great upliftment there. The whole atmosphere is surcharged with a sweet feeling of love. It affected me for a little while like an intoxicating drink. We were there for 3 nights. And the peculiarity of the place is that the tongue began to utter the name of the Lord without any attempt on my part. And it went on all the while except when I was sleeping. I thought what a blessed state it was. But as soon as I left the place, that intoxication was over.

Then we came to Allahabad. There is the confluence of two rivers, the Ganges and the Yamuna. Every six years there is a fair there [the Kumbha Mela], and monks of different orders,

pilgrims, and devotees meet and bathe at the confluence.
That period happened to come this year, and we were fortu-
nate to meet a gathering of at least two million people in one
place. We saw a procession of monks on elephants, horses,
and camels, and on foot. They were all dressed differently
according to the modes of different orders. And there was a
band of monks—completely naked and hundreds of them.
They had long matted hair and their bodies besmeared with
ash. Most of them are very pure souls. Funny thing, you can
never feel shocked though you see them completely naked.
Their physical forms were perfect and they looked neither
this way nor that way, but walked straight with the gait of
lions and their faces shining with a heavenly smile.

Now we are here, in the sacred city of Vishwanath, the
Lord of the Universe. This is such a place that though it is
very cold, you cannot sleep after 4 in the morning. One gets
into the meditative mood very easily. I am enjoying my stay
immensely. They observed Swamiji's birthday yesterday. There
will be public lectures next Sunday.

Two weeks later, Swami wrote Aparna once more from the
Ramakrishna Mission Home of Service at Varanasi:

We are still in Banaras, enjoying every moment of our stay
here. We go to the bank of the Ganges almost every afternoon, sit there, gaze at the river, and also meditate there
with hundreds of other devotees. I go to the temple [Vish-
wanath] every morning alone. Sometimes I have to push
my way through the crowd. And I like it. You can see
crowds with the fervor of devotion rushing to see and
touch the Lord. And everyone wants to go in first. Once
only as I was trying to get in with one crowd and another
crowd coming out, I was pushed back. I tried to pass the
door twice with flowers in one hand and Ganges water in
the other, and I was thrown back both times. So, helpless, I
was standing and watching and waiting for an opportunity
when the crowd would grow less. There came a priest, got

hold of my hand and said, "Swamiji, come with me." I said, "No, I like the crowd and I will go in through this door." He said, "You will have so much trouble to get in. Come with me." And he practically dragged me, took me through another secret door and placed me before the Lord.

Tomorrow we go to visit Sarnath, 7 miles from here, where Buddha gave his first sermon after his illumination. There had been a monastery there … which has been found out after an excavation. A new temple has been built. We hire a bus and take about 14 or 15 Swamis with us.

Swami and Sister attended Sri Ramakrishna's birthday celebration at Belur Math. Swami mentioned the festivities in a letter to Aparna: "The celebration on the 1st of March at the Math was a great success. There were 200,000 people gathered on the monastery grounds in the name of our master. Thirty thousand people were fed. In the evening there were fireworks."

Three days later, Swami and Sister arrived in Bhubaneswar. Swami wrote in his letter of March 4, 1936, to Aparna, "This is the monastery founded by Swami Brahmanandaji. Sister is the guest of a princess here, who lives next door to our monastery. We go to Puri on the 7th, and on the 9th we leave for Madras."

Swami Prabhavananda's last letter to Aparna on this pilgrimage was written from Madras on March 25, 1936. He wrote:

Tonight we leave for Colombo. On our way we shall visit some temples in southern India and expect to arrive in Colombo by the 2nd of April.

We visited Bangalore, Mysore, and the surrounding country. In Mysore we had an interview with His Highness the Maharaja. He is a very nice man and is devoted to our Mission. While coming from Mysore to Madras the train stopped in one station for more than half an hour, and some thirty devotees came to meet us at the station at 12 o'clock at night. They arranged for a meeting on the station platform. Imagine our embarrassment. Some passengers also alighted from the train to satisfy their curiosity. Police officers were moving around.

While having the interview with His Highness in Mysore, Sister did not realize that she was talking to His Highness. She thought he was His Highness' secretary. I sensed it, and at the first opportunity I addressed him as Your Highness. So Sister knew.

In later years, Swami sometimes talked about the holy places he had visited on this pilgrimage. One day he told us:

"In Conjeevaram, Sister and I went to the Shiva temple. Sister was not allowed to enter. While we were in the courtyard, a light came from the temple just to the place where we were standing, and struck us. With it there was a blissful vibration and a sound like a rumble of thunder. Both of us saw the light and felt a blissful presence. I walked in the path of the light to the temple, all the time feeling that blissful shock."

Swami Prabhavananda also described his darshan in the Jagannath Temple in Puri, in March 1936:

"We were going along the alley that leads behind the shrineroom. I felt a storm enveloping me. It was like being struck by a thunderbolt. For a moment I was afraid. If I had had my way, I would have cried, 'No!' Then I lost all consciousness of the outer world. I was overwhelmed. The temple, the crowd — everything vanished. Waves, waves, God, bliss. Surya [Swami Nirvanananda] said to the priest, 'Hold him.' That is all I remember. As I came nearer to the image, the experience became more intense. I remember hearing in English, 'God, God, God.' All light, waves of bliss. That's all I can describe. You can't describe the feeling. I got a glimpse. What I saw was formless."

In a postscript to a letter dated March 4, 1936, Swami wrote to Aparna, "The shrine especially made for Hollywood will reach you directly by freight." The reference is to the beautiful teakwood shrine in the Hollywood temple that was made in India during this pilgrimage according to Swami Prabhavananda's instructions. Swami often told us that the shrine was in his room at Belur Math before it was crated for shipping overseas.

Swamis Akhandananda and Vijnanananda came one after another to Swami Prabhavananda's room shortly before he left
the math. When he explained that he was taking the shrine to
America, each one blessed the shrine by standing before it and
touching it for a long time.

Plate 4. Swami Brahmananda, Madras, 1921

Plate 5. Sri Ramakrishna Math, Madras, 1921
1st row, 4th from l.: Swamis Shivananda and Brahmananda
2nd row, 7th from l.: Swami as Brahmachari Bhakti Chaitanya

Plate 6. Swami Prabhavananda, Hollywood, 1930s

Plate 7. Sister Lalita and Swami Prabhavananda, India, 1935

Plate 8. India pilgrimage, 1935
2nd row seated l. to r.: Swami Prabhavananda,
Swamis Virajananda and Akhandananda, and Sister Lalita

CHAPTER SEVEN

Later Years in Southern California

After Swami Prabhavananda's return from India in 1936, attendance at the lectures increased so much that it became difficult to accommodate the congregation in the Green House living room. Sister's savings, given to Swami ten years earlier, provided the means to build the Hollywood temple.

Swami said that Sister gave him $10,000. He consulted John Surbridge, a disciple whom he put in charge as contractor. The name of the architect was Monaco. Surbridge told Swami that the temple could be built for $8,000. It turned out that he could not finish the temple for this amount, and Swami did not want to take out a mortgage.

The very day that Swami thought of having the unfinished building boarded up until more funds were received, Dr. Kolisch, a new student, turned up. He not only gave the $2,500 needed to finish the temple but also provided funds for the chandeliers, other temple furnishings, and landscaping.

As for the pews, Swami related: "A woman devotee offered $4,000 and wrote a check. When her husband heard about it, he came and abused me. I told him to take the check back. He said, 'Oh, no, but we can't afford $4,000. What do you need?' Then he paid $2,500 for the pews."

Before the temple was constructed, Swami Prabhavananda had two experiences, which he often recalled:

"Before the Hollywood temple was built, I had a dream of Holy Mother. I saw her walking up the old front steps to the Green House living room.* She appeared living. I was standing with a crowd of people waiting to receive her. I was holding them back and said to them, 'Don't crowd Mother. Let her go to the living room.' But someone crossed in front of me and bowed down at her feet. Then I thought to myself, 'What, someone bows down to Mother before I do!' I prostrated before her and said, 'Jai Ma!' Then the dream broke, and I woke up."

Shortly after the temple was built, Swami Prabhavananda had a second experience of Holy Mother. He was then staying in a room off the Green House living room, in the northwest corner of the building. Swami told us, "I had a real vision of Holy Mother. I hadn't been thinking of her at all. I said to her, 'Mother, it is your grace.' She was in the standing posture, like in the picture on my desk [plate 9]. Solid power was emanating from her. She was looking at me graciously. The emotions with this vision were indescribable—joy, bliss! When the spell broke, I found myself sitting on my bed with tears of joy streaming down my face. The strange thing was that I had had no particular reverence for Holy Mother. Her grace is unconditional."

When Swami Prabhavananda's brother swamis came to Hollywood for the temple dedication in 1938, they objected to the shrine being connected with the auditorium. They were afraid that the public would not approve. Two of the swamis voiced objection to the ritual worship being done in such a public place where anyone could enter, but a third swami said, "What objection is there?"

In January 1940, the ten-item worship was introduced in the temple. A short form of the worship had been performed before that time.

Kali Puja was begun at the Hollywood temple in the early 1940s, using a framed picture of Mother Kali at Dakshineswar. Swami related:

---

* These steps were between the Green House and the present temple steps.

"After Kali Puja had been done for four or six years in Holly-wood by worshiping a photograph, Maharaj came to my room in Hollywood in spiritual vision. He said, 'Do the Kali Puja.' I answered, 'But there are not many days left, and it would not be possible to get an image from Calcutta.' Then I remembered, 'Khunki is in Santa Barbara. She can do the image.' He said, 'Yes.' I said I didn't want the boys and the girls to be together. But without saying anything Maharaj turned his thumbs down together, indicating to bring them together for the occasion. Then Maharaj went away. When I asked Khunki if she could do the image, she said yes. Khunki's image was used for the worship in 1948."

Kali Puja was performed in Hollywood [plate 10] several years before Shiva Ratri was begun. Swami Prabhavananda said that one night he could not sleep. Then he thought to himself, "If I can't sleep, why don't I do Shiva Ratri?"

———

About the coming of Gerald Heard, Aldous Huxley, and Chris-topher Isherwood, Swami said, "Gerald, Aldous, and Chris were pacifists. They got the addresses of the San Francisco and Los Angeles centers. They tried to find me but couldn't. Ivar Ave-nue did not go through to Hollywood Boulevard. One year lat-er [in 1939], I met Gerald by chance. Then he brought Aldous and Chris."

Many of Swami Prabhavananda's most important books were written in the 1940s and 1950s. Following are some statements made by Swami about his translations and original writings. He said that his Upanishads translation was based on the com-mentary of Shankara, and his Gita translation on the commen-taries of Shankara and of Madhusudana Saraswati.

Swami once made the statement that his favorite Upanishad was the Katha and his favorite chapters of the Gita were the sixth and the twelfth.

This is how Swami's translation of the Gita came about:

"Once I was away for a rest in Palm Springs. I had a Gita translation with me. When I read the twelfth chapter, I felt that the meaning had not been brought out; I saw deeper meaning in it. So I started to translate, and then Chris helped me. I translated and Chris edited. When Peggy Kiskadden came, she read what we had done and could not understand it. Then we went to Aldous. Chris read aloud, and Aldous listened. Aldous said, 'No, that is not right yet. Forget that Krishna is speaking to the Hindus in Sanskrit. Forget that this is a translation. Think that Krishna is speaking to an American audience in English.' Then Aldous told Chris which style to use for verse. Chris rewrote the whole eleventh chapter of the Gita, I think. He produced the book in a week. He was inspired."

While writing the life and teachings of Maharaj, Swami Prabhavananda had the following experience: "Every day while I was writing *The Eternal Companion*, I would get a fragrance." Not only Swami but others near him had the same experience.

Pravrajika Yogaprana remembered that the fragrance was perceptible in the Green House living room and beside the Hollywood temple. Pravrajika Prabhaprana remembered it near Swami's chair in the living room of the convent in Santa Barbara.

"When I translated the Bhagavatam [a well-known scripture about the life and times of Lord Krishna], I read the Psalms to get the rhythm of the verses. Then Dr. Manchester said, 'Your translation is not really verse, but you have created your own style.'"

Swami said that the commentary to *How to Know God* [a commentary of the *Yoga Sutras* of Patanjali] represents the essence of his knowledge. "After I finished writing *How to Know God*, I felt I had exhausted myself. I poured into that book whatever I knew." In July 1960, Swami said that the book should be rearranged according to subject matter.

The Spiritual Heritage of India was written in the 1930s, when Swami did not feel "pressed with too much work." Then the manuscript was lost for twenty years. Swami said he could never rewrite it; it was something he was able to do only as a young man. The manuscript was found in an unused cupboard in his living quarters in Hollywood during some remodeling.

Swami said about the book: "I am not a scholar. I would have had problems, so I used to pray to the Lord and ask him how it should be done. And I would get the inspiration and make notes. Later I sent my notes to a scholar, and the scholar said that everything was all right. That is how I wrote *The Spiritual Heritage of India*.

"Subrahmanya [V. S. Subrahmanya Iyer], Sarvepalli Radhakrishnan's teacher, went through the entire manuscript except the chapter on Ramakrishna. And he okayed everything. He was reader of philosophy at Mysore University and was reader to the Maharaja of Mysore. He made *Vedic Religion and Philosophy* [an early publication of Swami's] a textbook at Mysore University."

"I never think that I am going to give a lecture," Swami would tell us. "I always pray to Holy Mother, 'Mother, let me say words that will do good to these people.'

"Many times, even while I am lecturing, ideas have poured into me. Once in a class I said, 'Even the avatars [divine incarnations] have to have gurus.' Someone asked, 'Who was Christ's guru?' Out of my mouth came the words, 'John the Baptist.' I looked around to see who had spoken. Afterwards I thought, 'That's right.' Truth came out without my knowing it."

———

In 1942, Spencer Kellogg, a retired businessman, became interested in reading *The Gospel of Sri Ramakrishna*. He had visited the Trabuco College when Gerald Heard was there and was impressed. Swami Prabhavananda related:

"Then Mr. Kellogg bought the estate in Montecito and tried to make it something like an ashrama. He built the little shrine room. Nikhilananda was his guest. Sister and I went to bring Nikhilananda from Santa Barbara to Hollywood. That was the first time I met Mr. Kellogg. He made an appointment to see me in Hollywood, but when he came, he was with me in the office only for a moment, and then he left abruptly. I did not understand and thought I might have offended him unknowingly. Then Mr. Kellogg wrote that he wanted to be my disciple. He explained that something had happened to him in the office. He had become emotional; that is why he had left abruptly. In reply I wrote him that because he had met Nikhilananda first, I could not accept him as a disciple. He answered that Swami Nikhilananda was his friend, not his guru. I wrote to him that without Nikhilananda's permission I could not accept him as a disciple.

"One day we were celebrating the worship of the Divine Mother. I had finished the puja and almost everybody had gone. I was alone in the shrine when Mr. Kellogg came with a letter from Nikhilananda. Before I allowed him to speak, I said to him, 'Come and offer this flower to the Divine Mother.' He offered the flower and then gave me the letter. In the letter, Nikhilananda requested that I initiate Mr. Kellogg. In due course he was initiated. He wanted to help in the work here. He said he could offer $10,000 for our use. Afterward he called me up and wanted me to take the Santa Barbara property instead of the cash because his wife did not want to live in Santa Barbara. But I could not accept the property because we did not have money for its upkeep.

"Mr. Kellogg put his estate up for sale. He asked me to come and stay there during my vacation in July and August 1944, before it was sold. One day he invited some friends to meet me. He had lunch with us and then he was to go and bring his wife to the meeting. I noticed that his car was still parked in the driveway, and I wondered where he was. I found him sweeping in front of the little shrine. His back was turned toward me, and he did not see me. He was talking to himself, saying, 'Why should I sell Divine Mother's place? I don't need money. I will give the place to Swami.' And I answered, standing back of him, 'I accept it.' He threw away the broom, shook hands with me, and said, 'I will give you $10,000 a year as an endowment.' This was in August, and he told me he would make the deed of gift in January to facilitate his income tax. I agreed. He suddenly passed away in December, and we did not know what fate awaited us. In January, on Swamiji's birthday, a letter came from his lawyer or his bank, saying that he had willed the property and stocks to our Vedanta Society."

During the years following his meeting with Swami Prabhavananda, Gerald Heard had been organizing a college for religious students at Trabuco Canyon. As a result of his generous influence, the entire establishment was deeded to the Vedanta Society and was dedicated as the Ramakrishna Monastery in 1949.

And so the work expanded. While Swami Prabhavananda remembered with appreciation those who had devoted their services in any way or had offered their intellectual or material gifts, he always stressed that it is the Lord who brings his devotees and uses some of them as instruments in his work.

In connection with his view that he was only second in charge, that the work was divinely inspired and accomplished, Swami used to relate:

"When I first came to America, I had a dream. Swamiji came to me. He put his hands on my shoulders, pressed on them, and said, 'I want to see if you can carry my weight.'" Earlier, in Madras, Maharaj had told Swami, "Sri Ramakrishna does his own preaching. Be the witness." And Swami told us many times, "I really feel that I haven't done anything. And I could not have done anything. The Lord is doing everything."

Swami taught his disciples to welcome equally all who come to the Vedanta centers, saying, "Remember, whoever comes here is a child of God."

Plate 9. Sarada Devi, Calcutta, 1905

Plate 10. Kali Puja, Hollywood temple shrine, 1950
L. to r. Swamis Devatmananda and Prabhavananda, and Sarada performing the puja

Plate 11. Swami Prabhavananda, Aldous Huxley, Christopher Isherwood, at the Vedanta center, Hollywood

Plate 12. Sister Lalita and Swami Prabhavananda,
Santa Barbara convent, 1946

CHAPTER EIGHT

Final Days

EARLY IN 1976, Swami Prabhavananda asked for a photograph of Holy Mother, larger than the one that had stood on his desk for many years. When we inquired which pose he wanted, he chose from our photo album a seated, front-facing picture [plate 2]. There was an unusual intensity in the way he asked for it; we had it framed as soon as possible. When it was hung on the wall near Swami Brahmananda's picture above the mantel, Swami was very pleased. While eating his meals, he would sit silently and look from one picture to the other for a long time.

During the last months of his life, Swami related in detail much autobiographical material as well as stories about Sri Ramakrishna's direct disciples. He asked that several incidents pertaining to his stay in Mayavati and his pilgrimage to Kedar-Badri be noted down and gave instructions when and where they were to be published—after his death.* Swami seemed to realize that there was not much time left.

Swami made his last trip to Santa Barbara late in May 1976. One day he fell, which was a shock to his delicate system. On May 29, he was taken by ambulance to the hospital in Los Angeles and placed in the cardiac intensive care unit. His chronic congestive heart disease had worsened, and his weight was down to eighty pounds.

On June 1, Swami was transferred to a private room in the coronary care unit of the hospital. Toward evening, a wonderful mood came over him and continued to build. He repeated

---

* These incidents and Swami's instructions are included in chapter three.

several names of God and a verse from "Prakritim" [a hymn to Sarada Devi by Swami Abhedananda]. Speaking alternately in Bengali and English, he also mentioned the names of Swamis Shivananda, Turiyananda, Abhedananda, Saradananda, Vijnan-ananda, and Adbhutananda—all of whom he had known. He repeated Maharaj's statement, "Light, more light; is there any end to it?" And he recalled Swami Turiyananda's and Swami Sadananda's predictions that he would go and work in America.

Shortly after six in the evening, Swami asked that his monastic disciples be called. They came from Hollywood, Santa Barbara, and Trabuco, and entered his hospital room in twos to receive his final instructions. Those who discussed this evening afterward agreed that they had never seen Swami in such an extraordinary mood. A special radiance and power shone through his frail, almost transparent body. His facial expression was joyful. The following is a composite of what some disciples heard him say.

In the presence of two monastics, Swami said, "Ananda mrityu [this blissful death]." With a strong and clear voice he chanted a mantra loudly and asked them to join him.

Then Swami asked, "Do you remember, 'Swing low, sweet chariot'?" He seemed to be referring to the idea of a chariot coming for the departing soul.

Swami spoke of Thakur, Sarada Devi, and Shakti [Primal Energy, the power of Brahman] in Bengali. Then he translated, "Thakur and Ma are like fire and its power to burn; they are inseparable."

To someone else, Swami said, "Remember, we are nobodies. There is only Thakur, Ma, Swamiji, Maharaj."

To one nun, he said, "Worship, worship, and worship, and you will have bliss and greater bliss"; to another, "Always make japam"; to a third, "Always serve the Lord; it is his work you are doing." He reassured one of the brahmacharis, "Maharaj has taken care of this ashrama for many years, and he will continue to do so." He told one monastic, "You will be liberated, and

and by the grace of Maharaj seven generations up and down your family will be blessed." And he said to another, "Remember, I will love you always." To a disciple who was weeping, Swami said, "Don't weep. I will be with you always."

One disciple reported that Swami had told her, "I am not able to see my householder disciples." She said, "Surely they will feel your blessings." Swami replied, "They are blessed and they will all be liberated." Among the householder devotees, Krishnamurti [Dr. Riccitelli] and Abhaya [Swami's disciple and nurse] were at the hospital that day.

Swami's extraordinary mood and behavior made us wonder whether he would survive the night. The next day, however, he returned to his normal state. But he remembered that he had said something significant to each person present the evening before.

On June 6, Swami was moved out of the cardiac care unit to a regular hospital room. The next morning he complained, "I have had so many real visions, and yet I am suffering. Why? Can you tell me?" To one of his new nurses, he said, "Ralph, you will have to suffer with us."

On June 18, he was brought home to the Hollywood center by ambulance, and professional nurses took care of him around the clock. Although he was very weak, he began to walk a little in his room.

On June 21, at breakfast time, Swami asked, "Is it July 1?" Ralph, who was on duty at the time, replied, "No, it is June 21." A little later Swami broke the silence again and asked, "Are there thirty days in June?" And someone who was in the room answered, "Yes."

On June 24, Swami told the disciple who brought his supper, "Do you know what happened today? I began to get a fragrance. Abhaya was here, and we both got a fragrance. Then I felt the presence of Maharaj, and I asked him, 'Maharaj, have you come to take me?'"

The last five days of his life, Swami came down the steps from his room, supported—or rather, half carried—by Swami Krishnananda and one of the nurses. Each day he walked a bit farther, and on the last day, July 3, he circumambulated the entire temple.

In the afternoon of July 3, Swami had a heart attack. His breathing was labored, and he told a disciple that he was dying. When she began to repeat the Lord's name softly, he stopped her, saying, "Not yet." He said that he did not want to go to the hospital again. The Santa Barbara convent and Trabuco monastery were informed, and as his condition became critical, the devotees were called, some of whom kept vigil in the temple during the evening.

Around 10 p.m., Swami said six times, "Jai Bhagavan, Jai Maharaj." Then, very softly, he added in Bengali, "Maharaj will come." When Swami Chetanananda [the assistant minister] asked Swami whether he was suffering, Swami answered, "I have not suffered at all."

At 11:15 p.m., Swami Prabhavananda asked his nurse what time it was. When he was told, he said, "No, too soon, too soon. It must be midnight." Frequently during the day he had asked the time.

At 11:55 p.m., we were summoned to Swami's bedside. As we came into the room, for a moment it seemed that Swami had already made the transition. His shining eyes were gazing upward and far into the distance. But then we realized that his lips were still moving in repetition of the Lord's name.

The room was silent, holding no sense of impending death, but of a blissful peace. Swami's breathing was so easy and smooth that most of us could not be sure when it had stopped. While we were chanting "Hari Om Ramakrishna," he entered into mahasamadhi. At 12:03 a.m., on the Bicentennial Fourth of July 1976, Swami went to Maharaj.

Plate 13. Swami Prabhavananda, September 1959

Plate 14. Swami Prabhavananda, Hollywood center

Part Two: In the Swami's Own Words

CHAPTER NINE

In Conversation

SWAMI: I HAVE no fear of death any more. When I had that operation [for hernia in 1950], I had to sign away my life [a release
required by the hospital]. For two days after that I was in terror.
I tried to reason, to make japa—nothing helped. Finally I prayed
to Maharaj. He took the fear away immediately—just like that!
    DISCIPLE: And the fear never came back?
    SWAMI: No, never. (1/1959)

To monastics at the breakfast table, Thanksgiving Day, 1952: "I
don't want you to become just saints; I want you to be such
that you can produce saints."

Swami always gave a great deal of freedom to those who
served him or the Vedanta Society in any capacity. When Lu-
tah Riggs was hired in 1955 as the architect for the Santa Barbara temple, she told Swami that she had never been in a
church she liked. Swami said to her, "I give you carte blanche
to build one that you do like." His trust brought out the best in
her; the temple she designed won first prize in the Santa Barbara Civic Awards of 1956.

DISCIPLE: Swami, how was the atmosphere at Ridgely Manor?*
SWAMI: I can't really say. In order to know, I would have to sit

* Swami Vivekananda had been a guest at Ridgely Manor, the Leggetts' country
home in New York State.

down and meditate. Shankara, for instance, would pass by a place and say, "A great soul must be living here." But I am not that advanced. I must sit down and calm my mind. But, through the grace of my guru and Mother, I can raise my consciousness whenever I want to. (1956)

"The first step is 'I am His.' The last is 'He belongs to me'; I don't know yet what that means." (1956)

The possibility of building a larger temple in Hollywood was under discussion. Swami said, "Swami Prakashananda taught me, 'Never go into debt for anything.' If the Lord wants something done, let him provide the means to get it done." (1/1962)

"'Vanity of vanities, all is vanity' except to love God [Ecclesiastes 1:2]. I am beginning to understand this now." (11/1962)

"Still I have the inclination to live in Almora or in Kankhal or in Banaras—just live there and meditate and study and think of the Lord and weep for the Lord. But my health won't permit it. If I spent money and got a nice room ... but it isn't so easy." (12/9/1962)

"I am attached to my children [affectionate term for disciples]; I certainly found that out. Whenever I have had thoughts of going away and leaving you, I have never had any assent from Maharaj. I would worry what would happen to you."

A disciple was telling Swami how thrilling it was to see the growth of the Vedanta work at this time—so many people asking for appointments and taking out memberships. Swami said, "I will tell you girls, this life is wonderful. Now that this old body is going, crowds are coming. And greater things will happen."

DISCIPLE: Swami, what do you mean?

SWAMI: This is Sri Ramakrishna's age. Great crowds will come. (1960s)

"The Eternal among the noneternals, the Fulfiller of all desires—right desires—[is the Lord]. I want nothing for myself. I just want to see that his work is firmly established. That is my only desire." (11/1966)

"I have no dispassion, no devotion, no renunciation. But what grace I have—without rhyme or reason!" (Easter Sunday, 1968)

After Swami recovered from his heart attack in 1966, he began to attend morning meditation in the Hollywood temple again. One day he was quite exhausted, and someone suggested that he rest in his room instead of going to the temple for morning meditation. Swami replied, "You don't know what joy I find in that meditation. I can't give it up." (5/18/1970)

Swami, speaking of his personal meditation routine, said one day, "Generally, every morning from 4:30 to 6:30 I go through a process of thinking of Thakur, Mother, Maharaj, and Swamiji, all the direct disciples, and all the holy places I have visited. Sometimes I drop off to sleep, and then I wake up again and continue."

Swami said he thinks every day of Swamis Akhandananda and Vijnanananda touching the teakwood shrine he showed them in India before bringing it to Hollywood in 1936. He said the two direct disciples stood touching the roof of the shrine, each for an hour.

Swami told us that he chants Ram Nam every night before going to sleep—first the pranam mantra, "Om Sri Sita, Lakshmana, Bharata, Shatrughna" then "Nanya Spriha," and three verses from "Shuddha Brahma."

One day there was a discussion about the Hollywood shrine. Suddenly Swami said, with a disgusted look on his face, "When you speak of deities, it gives me a shiver. These are not pictures; they are living!"

Then Swami proceeded to tell the following incident, which

had taken place years earlier. "I was doing the worship in the Hollywood shrine. While I was bathing and wiping Thakur's picture, the picture became alive—color and everything. I was not in any special mood. I looked around. I was conscious. I looked again. It was living for about five minutes. Thakur was peeping behind the glass."

When we questioned Swami, he said that the face became three-dimensional. "The photograph disappeared, as it were. I was conscious only of the face and the glass. No ecstasy, no feeling accompanied the experience; it was in normal consciousness. I began to doubt myself; that is why I looked around. I pinched myself to see if it was real. Thakur had a glowing face; he was beautiful!" (9/27/1973)

"Sometimes I feel, why bother about relics? The living Lord is here [pointing to his heart]. But relics remind us of the truth that he is dwelling in us."

Disciple: Swami, do you ever wish for those early days—just a few intimate devotees, no problems of a large organization?

Swami: No. Our Lord didn't come for just a few, but for the whole world—for the good of the many, for the happiness of the many.

A swami's life is dedicated to the service of God and mankind. No, I love people; that is my temperament. With the last breath Holy Mother taught, "No one is a stranger. Everyone is your own." Those who come to the house of the Lord—there is something in them.

In the course of a conversation Swami remarked, "When Maharaj comes back again, I want to come with him."

Disciple: Those who come back are very unselfish.

Swami: Why?

Disciple: So much trouble!

Swami: Only the body suffers.

Then Swami said, "All the disciples of Thakur will come back again."

During the same conversation Swami said, "Guru and *ishta* [chosen ideal] become one. Do you understand?"

DISCIPLE: I have read and heard about it, but I haven't experienced it yet.

SWAMI: To me, Maharaj and Thakur are one and the same.

"I have seen gods and goddesses walking on earth. And what do I have now? Only a memory. But one thing I have—I feel that Maharaj is with me most of the time." (4/15/1976)

"Maharaj gave me everything."

"All the excitement is on the surface. Underneath I am a speck of dust of Maharaj's feet. That is my real nature."

CHAPTER TEN

Meditation

"THE KINGDOM OF God is within you." The sea of consciousness lies centered in every heart. In this sea of consciousness there are infinite aspects of God. Whichever aspect you remember at the moment, that aspect becomes present immediately within you. So when you worship Rama, know that it is Rama that fills this sea of consciousness in the depths of your own being. Or, when you think of Mother Kali, know that it is she alone who dwells within. To think of God is to see God—for his presence abides forever and ever within your own heart.

(Note to a disciple)

———

As you sit for meditation, bow down to Sri Ramakrishna, the living master of the age, and repeat this prayer:

O Lord, may I serve thee in every way.
Whatever I do, whatever I give,
   may I do and give as an offering unto thee.
May I be truly an instrument in thy hands.
Thou art Sri, the Mother of all happiness and bliss.
Do thou come as Sri, the Goddess of Fortune, to me.
May I be a glory among men.
May I be superior to the riches.
May I enter into thee, and may thou, O Lord,
   enter into me.
Purified am I by thy touch, O Lord of my heart.

Thou art my only refuge.
Enlighten me, for I am thine, O Lord.

Then feel that you are free and rest in the peace and bliss that come in meditation. Repeat toward the north, south, east, and west: "Let every being be peaceful. Let every being be blissful." Send love and goodwill to every being on every plane and every sphere: "May peace come to all beings. May all seek the higher life, and may they all reach the goal."

Think of your teacher, your guru: feel love for him and pray, "May the Lord protect us both. May there be no dispute between us, and may our study be illumined."

Feel the presence, protection, and guidance of Krishna, Buddha, Christ, Ramakrishna, and all the great teachers of the world. "May they inspire me with love, truth, and purity; and may they in mercy lead me higher; for none ask in vain who ask sincerely."

Repeat: "I meditate on the glories of that Being who has produced this universe. In him we live, move, and have our being. May he enlighten my mind."

Pray to your conception of God (your ishta or chosen ideal). Pray:

Lead kindly Light, amidst the encircling gloom, lead thou me on!

Show me thy ways, O Lord; teach me thy paths. Lead me in thy truth and teach me, for thou art the God of my salvation; in thee do I wait all the day.

The Lord is my shepherd; I shall not want. He maketh me to lie down in green pastures; he leadeth me beside the still waters. He restoreth my soul; he leadeth me in the paths of righteousness for his name's sake. Yea, though I walk through the valley of the shadow of death, I will fear no evil, for thou art with me; thy rod and thy staff they comfort me. Thou preparest a table before me in the presence of mine enemies;

thou anointest my head with oil; my cup runneth over. Surely goodness and mercy shall follow me all the days of my life and I will dwell in the house of the Lord forever. (Psalm 23)

Then think of the mind as pure and perfect and that all your thoughts tend Godward, to truth and purity, and no evil can enter your mind.

Your one ideal of life is to realize God within, to realize unity with the infinite; to be perfect even as the Father in heaven is perfect. Repeat:

I am Life. My glory is like the mountain peak. The light of my knowledge and purity spreads far and wide; I am truly immortal. I am the brightest wealth. I am wise, immortal, and imperishable.

I am that infinite ocean of knowledge, existence, and bliss absolute. I am beyond time, space, and causation. I am one with every being, one with the Infinite. I am He, the great light whose form is like ethereal essence, whose Self is truth, perfect peace, and immortality, who is the solace of my life, the bliss of my mind.

I cannot want, nor can I be miserable. For the fullness of life is within me; the infinite power and eternal power and eternal bliss are within me.

Then think of the body as a temple of God. Think it is as strong and healthy in every organ, every function, every limb, in every tissue. No disease can enter the body. No impurity can be there. No accident can befall it. It is the best instrument I have to attain the goal. With the help of this body, I will cross the ocean of life, of maya, and arrive safely on the shores of re-alization—samadhi.

Then concentrate the mind on the surface of the body, beginning at the toes, and follow the surface of the body. Pass upward bit by bit until you reach the head, holding each perfect, lacking nothing. Then hold the whole perfect, an instrument given to you by God to enable you to attain Truth.

Then fix the mind on the center in the forehead or in the lotus of the heart, whichever appeals to you, and think of the light as the light of your own soul, God.

Then let the mind run as it wills for ten minutes while you stand as a witness and watch the working of your own mind. Do not seek to control it even if the thoughts are bad and impure. It is only when we know what we think that we can control it. At first you will find you have a thousand thoughts about everything. After a while, you will find the number and variety of thoughts will grow fewer. Then take a hold of the mind with a firm hand, grasp it tightly with all the determination of which you are capable; concentrate your mind on your highest ideal, your conception of God [the chosen ideal]; seem to see that ideal, to hear the voice of that ideal; to become one with the ideal. (Repeat the mantra as you meditate.)

Om, Peace, Peace, Peace.

SWAMI: In meditation you should think of your chosen ideal as luminous and that his light is illuminating everything. Think of him as living and conscious. As you continue meditating thus on the form of the chosen ideal, the form will gradually melt into the formless, the infinite. Then will come a vivid sense of the living presence. Finally, the eye of wisdom opens, and he is directly perceived. Ah! That's another realm, beyond this universe! This universe appears as nothing. The mind then is dissolved and there is the experience of *savikalpa* samadhi [communion with God in which the distinction of "I" and "thou" remains].

Next comes the realization of *nirvikalpa* samadhi—the Absolute union. That experience is beyond thought and speech. Nothing to be seen! Nothing to be heard! Infinite, Infinite alone! This is a matter of direct experience.

You could not be here without the Lord's grace. When you come to our Lord, this is your last birth. At the moment of death the Lord will give you a hit, and the darkness will go and there will be light. At least that you can expect.

DISCIPLE: But, Swami, I want that before death!

SWAMI: Then struggle for it.

———

"When you go to meditate, first think: God *is*. Convince yourself of this. Then think how he must look, and remember he loves you. Those who feel his love become humble and feel they can never love like that. His love is so great that he doesn't let us know how he loves us."

About the *anahata* sound Om: "This is the cosmic sound; it is not caused by one object striking another as are ordinary sounds. In meditation when one is a little absorbed one may hear first the ringing of bells, etc., and then finally the sound Om which is the anahata sound. This is one of the lower experiences. To see light is much higher. It is not merely just seeing light but also experiencing a current of bliss. It strikes you with an ocean of light and waves of bliss—wonderful. But how can I explain it to you; mere words do not describe it!"

"You don't always have the vision of what you are meditating on. So you will know it is not self-hypnosis. He may appear to you in another form, because they [various aspects of the Divine] are all one and the same, yet separate. They are eternally existing."

"Just as fire and heat cannot be separated, so Master and Mother cannot be separated. Think of the one or the other, or think of both—it is all the same." (From a letter to a disciple, 1/16/1953)

"When you are trying to meditate and pray, trying to realize God, but you don't see him, feel that he is watching you and is aware that you are making the attempt to realize him. That is very important."

———

"Samadhi, ecstasy, spiritual visions—these are of varying degrees. They are not all the same. They indicate different levels of growth. To have visions of Mother is a wonderful thing—indicates direct grace. But that is not enough. To be intimate with her, to talk to her—these again are greater and higher. 'Light, more light, more light!' There is no end to this. Yes, we need only strive for constant awareness and must always pray for love, pure love for her blessed feet. Love ultimately is the supreme goal—love that is identical with perfection and immortal bliss." (From a letter to a disciple, 11/1/1955)

"It is very good to feel the all-pervading presence and feel that present everywhere. This is not *imagination*, but it is the feeling of the reality. For, in fact, *that* is pervading and permeating every being and thing, nay, *that* is the only reality. Beings and things are only waves of name and form on the bosom of the reality.

"But this reality, or God, will still remain an abstraction until you can see that in your own soul. And for that end it is very necessary that you meditate on the Master as a concrete form, a real spiritual form of that all-pervading existence. See him within the shrine of your heart. See him as the soul of your soul and as the soul of all beings and things. See him, talk to him; feel him as your own—that you belong to him and he belongs to you.

"This practice of meditation on him within the shrine of your heart is very important. Through this practice alone the abstraction will not remain an abstraction but will become a living reality. Of course, the mind will find difficulty to meditate—but force it again and again. Do not let it go the easy way. Through practice, however, not only will it be easy, but such joy will overflow from within that it will be overwhelming." (From a letter to a disciple, 12/29/1938)

"When, through continued regular practice, habit is formed, then there flows the current Godward. Then it is that all our problems are solved. Problems may arise, but they dissolve away with the current of our mind flowing Godward.

"Yes, the only thing that we must ask of him is to have more and more love for him. Everything else is a vanity.

"Do not have any doubt. As you think of the Lord and pray to him, your inner mind will be shown the way, and it cannot go wrong. Yes, Ramakrishna is within us, and we are also in Ramakrishna. 'We live, work, and have our being in him.'

"Practice! Practice! Practice! See for yourself. Then is it that all doubts dissolve away." (From a letter to a disciple, 12/6/1953)

"Practice japa more and more, and you are sure to find the inexpressible joy—the joy that knows no limit. Until you are established in that there will be ups and downs. But do not lose heart. The days you feel dry within need more strenuous struggle to meditate. You may not come out of the dryness while you are striving—but as an aftereffect of that you will see how your whole being is responding to the bliss of God—even when you are not expecting it." (From a letter to a disciple, 7/2/1941)

––––––––

"People come to me and say their prayers, but don't go high enough. No, you must feel that he is aware, he is listening. Before your prayer has even entered your mind, he knows about it."

"See God in all manifestations; where else would you see him?"

"See him everywhere. He is consciousness in all beings. We use his consciousness when we think, move, or speak. And not just insignificant consciousness of self, but infinite. 'Thou art that,' a guru tells his disciple. The ego is insignificant, but not the Self—Atman."

"The guru sees Brahman in his disciple. When the disciple can see Brahman in his guru, he becomes a guru [meaning illumined]."

"Tell the Lord: 'I can't see you; I can't meditate. You know all this. Please let me keep my mind in you.' Talk to the Lord. It does help." (1958)

"Meditate as though Yama, the god of Death, is standing at your back."

"Don't think of God as so great and powerful. Feel that he is your very own. That is adoration."

"Nonattachment is not indifference but is attachment solely to God."

"To surrender to God is to think of him often."

"To be desireless—what does this mean? It means to yearn intensely for God."

"A holy man is humble. He does not assert himself."

"Make japa. The Lord is consciousness. Here [pointing to his head and heart] is consciousness; the Lord's name is consciousness."

"The high court won't take your case unless you go to the lower court first [God won't grant your prayers unless you surrender to your guru first]."

"The Lord never fails if you ask him sincerely for anything. I can tell you that."

"The Lord is dwelling in you. Learn to dwell in him. The Lord is the Lord of our life, the ground of our existence."

"Sometimes when you meditate, think that you will be completely destroyed unless you keep your mind in God. That intensifies your concentration. Don't stay on the surface. Dive deep."

"The ideal way to chant the name of the Lord is with faith in the guru's words, with devotion, and with concentration on the meaning of the mantra. But if you can't do that, make japa mechanically. The name of the Lord will sink into your subconscious mind that way."

"The mind is a rascal mind. You think you are concentrating it on the Lord, but suddenly it has run away. Struggle. Keep struggling to bring it back. I'll tell you a secret. Be aware as you go to meditate that the Lord is seated in your heart. That is no imagination; it is reality. When you have his vision you will realize that he knew all the time—that he accepted all you offered him."

"There is a great difference between human love and divine love."

"Someone may do many good deeds and a few bad ones, and man remembers the bad. But you can neglect God, and he will remember the few times that you thought of him."

"Do you know how you should study the scriptures? Read four or five lines and meditate on them. Then try to live the truths expressed in those lines for a few days."

"Religion is simple. God is simple. And if you are simple, you find God."

"Faith, faith is the root!"

"Perfect faith is perfect knowledge."

"All you need to know is that God *is*; that he is within, and that you can find him. Then forget all the rest. If we can only have that faith that he is here and that he is listening."

DISCIPLE: Even if you were able to think of the Lord all the time, wouldn't it be a strain?

SWAMI: Yes, sometimes you think of him and think of him. He is with you all the time. The mind gets tired.

DISCIPLE: Can you stop then?

SWAMI: Yes, you can. You can even read the newspaper [to relax the mind]. Then again you want to think of the Lord; and that sweetness comes, and you want to think of him more and more.

SWAMI: When it comes to God, whatever you have achieved if you once find him—or the inner growth you have achieved even if you don't find him—remains with you; it cannot be taken away. Your character, your achievement, stays with you.

CHAPTER ELEVEN
Spiritual Ideals

"UNLESS YOU HAVE the Lord and Mother, life is empty. You have them, they're looking at you—just remember that the Lord and Mother are looking at you, children. They are looking at you and in good time they'll reveal themselves to you. Surrender yourself to the Lord and Mother. You have no friend but the Lord and Mother.

"Maharaj told me that—that their love is so great that they don't dare show it, don't let you know that they love you. That's the fact—they love us. Thakur knows us, Mother knows us, Swamiji knows us, Maharaj knows us—and they know every moment of our life. They're patient and they wait, and they give us a slap now and then correcting us; but their love never fails. When I feel even a little of that, I just can't stand it and weep.

"We don't know how to love the Lord. We feel that we love the Lord, but just let us feel that the Lord loves us—that's enough. Nothing else matters. The Lord knows us and he's looking after us. You don't have to do a thing about it. Just feel it. No willpower there. Just let go and feel his love, that's enough. That will carry you on. There's nothing higher than that."

"You have come within the orbit. Never fear. You are on the train. Stay on it and you will reach your destination."

DISCIPLE: Swami, what is your definition of spiritual life?

SWAMI: Spiritual life is to forget yourself and to make God the center of your heart. I was just thinking this evening, "With whom did I live? Was it possible?" Your own parents leave you; and after they have died, you forget. But these disciples [of Sri Ramakrishna]—time passes, and they are nearer and nearer to you. Our relationship with our family is a temporary relationship. Our eternal relationship is with God. That is what this is. It is the real relationship; it is for eternity. (1/26/1963)

DISCIPLE: How are we to take refuge in the Lord?

SWAMI: Jesus said, "Abide in me and I in you" [John 15:4]. If we can follow this one teaching, we will become illumined souls. Krishna said the same thing: "Lodge your mind in me. Thus you shall dwell in me. Do not doubt it, here and hereafter" [Bhagavad Gita 12.18].

"Today this thought came to me: A worldly person, knowing famous people, will be very proud. In every conversation he will bring up that he knows So-and-so. But when you know God, the Emperor of emperors, you become humble." (2/21/1962)

"Does religion depend absolutely on an avatar? Take away Christs and Buddhas and Ramakrishnas! Take away all philosophy and theology and scriptures—still the truth of eternal religion will be there, because the kingdom of God is within. Each human soul is divine. Find it! Realize it! Seek your own Self! Find your own Self, and you will find God—call him Christ, Buddha, Krishna, Ramakrishna, or whatever you will." (From a letter to a disciple)

"Whatever you gain in spiritual life, you can never lose. It may remain covered. You may seem to retrogress, but you will find that you are beginning again where you left off. That is the beauty of spiritual achievement."

"What you wish to achieve, practice that as a discipline [discipline in the sense of *sadhana*]." (7/1967)

"At the beginning of the ritual worship, you touch the eyes, ears, nose, and mouth. What does it mean? To close the doors of the senses. In the same way, when you go to meditate, think that you are closing the doors of the senses. Then make your mind blank for a moment; don't think or concentrate. And then gather the forces of the mind and begin your meditation." (9/1958)

"In the path of God there is no need to be discouraged, there is no failure."

"My master said, 'Even one moment that you think of God is a blessed moment.' Everyone is afraid. The world is full of fear. There is only one way to come out of fear, and that is to take refuge in God." (6/1962)

Disciple: Do holy people worry?

Swami: I know from my own case. When I told Maharaj I was going away to practice austerities, he got so worried. He said, "Call Tarak-da [Swami Shivananda]!" as if he couldn't control me. I never saw my father so worried about me. Of course, it was because Maharaj thought that if I left I would be ruined.

"Let Mother work things out for you. Do not worry and fret, but rest peacefully, surrendering yourself and your problems to her. She knows best, and she always does the right thing by us.

"My answer to all problems is, 'Make japa.' It is a simple answer, but I know definitely that it works." (From a letter to a disciple, 7/1952)

"As soon as you receive the mantra from the guru, you are no longer a human being. You have become God." (5/5/1973, Swami quoting from the Mahanirvana Tantra)

"Prayer is a wonderful thing, and the Lord listens to every prayer. If you want to help anyone, pray for that person. It does work—wonderfully!"

DISCIPLE: What good does it do to pray for others? Doesn't the Lord know everything? Isn't he all merciful?

SWAMI: Yes, the Lord knows everything. Justice is meted out according to karma. But what does prayer do? It wipes out karma. When you are really penitent, he listens.

DISCIPLE: Isn't that petitionary prayer?

SWAMI: Is there anything wrong with petitionary prayer? In the Gita you read that there are four classes of people who seek God. Sri Krishna says that all of them are noble.* There is nothing wrong with petitionary prayer. Later, when you find a little sweetness in God, you feel, "Lord, I don't want anything but you."

On another occasion Swami said that Maharaj had taught him to pray only for two things: devotion and knowledge.

"A man was seriously ill. He was the only support of his sister. This sister went to Maharaj and begged him again and again to save her brother. Maharaj asked us to find the mantra of a certain deity. We tried and tried, but we could not find it in the books. I have forgotten whether Maharaj wanted us to make japa of that mantra or whether he wanted the sister to make japa. Anyway, we could not find the mantra. The man died. The next day I opened the prayer book, and there was the mantra!

"No, I could never use that mantra to avert someone's death. What good would it do? What kind of a life would that person lead if he lived—do we have any idea?"

Sudhira, one of Swami Prabhavananda's earliest disciples, said that around 1937 she was living at the Vedanta Society in Hollywood. She was then working as a nurse at a hospital. While taking care of a patient who was seriously ill, Sudhira became depressed. One day, Swami asked her what was wrong. She told him that this patient was suffering. Things were happening in the hospital that shouldn't have. It wasn't fair. Swami said to Sudhira, "People have a right to their pain and suffering. Don't try to remove it. Sustain and comfort."

* See Bhagavad Gita 7.16.

"It does not pay to be overly zealous. Constant recollectedness is a state of attainment. You have to have patience and perseverance. It doesn't work just to go back home and try to practice constant recollectedness all at once. You have to go slowly and patiently and persevere. Begin, say, with half an hour a day. Then increase. Later you will come to a stage of growth when you can't help yourself: the thought of God comes all the time. The 'Hound of Heaven' takes possession of you. You don't become a saint in a day. Patanjali says, 'Practice becomes firmly grounded when it has been cultivated for a long time, uninterruptedly, with earnest devotion' [*Yoga Sutras* 1.14]. The main thing is, you have to struggle sincerely."

Swami: Swamiji said, "Work is worship." Maharaj used to say, "Work is worship; work and worship." If you don't work, you can't meditate. To work for the Lord isn't attachment. It is nonattachment.

Disciple: But Swami, I shouldn't go on thinking about my work when I go to the shrine room! I have to be able to drop it, don't I?

Swami: That is the ideal—to be intensely attached to what you are doing while you are doing it. Swamiji used to say, "Attach yourself and detach yourself at a moment's notice." (1/2/1954)

"Nonattachment is not indifference. It is selfless love."

We had a talk with Swami about how Sri Chaitanya died. Swami said that Khoka Maharaj believed that Sri Chaitanya threw himself in the ocean at Puri. The blue water reminded him of Krishna. His body was never recovered. Swami also told us that according to another version, Sri Chaitanya became merged in the deity in a temple near Puri.

Swami Prabhavananda's translation of the Buddhist mantra "Om Mani Padme Hum": "Meditating on the Jewel (of God) in the lotus (of the heart)."

Swami said that the Song of Solomon expressed the *madhura bhava* [the sweet mood].

He explained that Christ's words on the cross, "My God, my God, why hast thou forsaken me?" did not mean that Christ had reverted to his human side. Christ was quoting the beginning of the 22nd Psalm. Swami said, further, that Christ was always "the ripe coconut," referring to Sri Ramakrishna's comparison of the illumined soul to a dry coconut whose kernel had loosened from the shell after the milk had dried up. Similarly, the illumined soul has realized that body and soul are separate. The mind of such a perfected being does not identify with the pleasure or pain of the body.

CHAPTER TWELVE

Recollections

SWAMI SHANKARANANDA HEARD Swami Brahmananda quote Ramakrishna: "I am the French possession." Swami Prabhavananda said that "the French possession" means "the sanctuary." Swami Prabhavananda explained that if you escaped from British India and went to the French possession, "the British couldn't touch you there."

"Sri Ramakrishna said about himself: 'I am he who wipes out karma [*kapala mochana*].'"

Swami Prabhavananda also repeated the following statement by Sri Ramakrishna: "Whoever thinks of me will find everything."

Swami heard directly from Swamis Premananda and Turiyananda that they did not agree with Swami Saradananda's view of the avatar as expressed in *Sri Ramakrishna: The Great Master*. Swami Saradananda believed that the avatar forgets his divinity and that his struggle for the vision of God is real. Swamis Premananda and Turiyananda believed that the avatar is always conscious that he is God and that he has a mission; his behavior as a human being is merely play-acting.* In this connection, Swami Prabhavananda told the story of Swami Turiya-

---

* None of the monastic disciples doubted Sri Ramakrishna's avatarhood. However, this passage exemplifies an unusual breadth of viewpoints within a religious tradition, showing that, at the highest level, there is room for deeply considered perspectives at variance even amongst the direct disciples of Sri Ramakrishna.—*Ed.*

the latter complained about his throat [pain], and that Sri Rama-krishna had then remarked, "Ah, the rascal has found me out!"

In the evening in his room, Swami Prabhavananda mentioned that Swamis Vivekananda and Brahmananda did not want Sri Ramakrishna's miracles published. But a couple of his miracles are published in *Sri Ramakrishna: The Great Master*: In the first miracle, Ramakrishna had made a white and red hibiscus blos-som on the same stem to show to Mathur Babu. In the second miracle, when fatally ill with cancer and hardly able to move, he was seen running down into the garden to protect the young disciples from a cobra. Holy Mother witnessed this.

Swami Prabhavananda did not remember the source of the fol-lowing miracle. It probably pertained to Kalipada Ghosh:

"Once the wife of an alcoholic came to Sri Ramakrishna and begged him to free her husband from his addiction to drink. All their money had gone into his drinking. Sri Ramakrishna sent her to Holy Mother. Holy Mother sent her back to Sri Rama-krishna. Sri Ramakrishna again sent her to Holy Mother, as these two would sometimes do. It was part of their divine play. This time, Holy Mother gave the woman a vilva leaf [sacred to Shiva] and asked her to touch her husband with it. The woman did, but for months nothing happened. Then one day, the man walked into Sri Ramakrishna's room. Thakur said to him, 'I have been waiting for you.'

"'Can you give me a drink of wine?'

"'I will give you a better drink than that.' With these words, Thakur went into ecstasy. His ecstasy communicated itself to the man, and they both danced together. The man, of course, was transformed." (6/12/1963)

"At one time Maharaj was sitting in a corner of Thakur's room, noting down his teachings. Thakur asked him, 'Rakhal, what are you doing?'

"'I am noting down your teachings.'

"Thakur told him, 'Stop that and listen!'

"Then Maharaj said to us, 'I was not clever enough. I should not have listened to him!'"

"I heard the following directly from Maharaj. When he wrote *Words of the Master*, he wrote what he remembered. He had forgotten much. Then he would meditate, and Thakur would come to him and repeat many things. Thakur did not want Maharaj to publish two teachings, but Maharaj told us that he found one of them already published by Swami Saradananda. It is the teaching that those who die in Banaras attain liberation and that Kali comes and cuts the knots of bondage."*

"When I went to India in 1949, I met an old man in Vishnupur. He had heard about us and came one day with many kinds of sweets. We asked him why he came to see us. He said that he had met Sri Ramakrishna and had wanted to see me because I was a monk in his order. Then he began his story:

"His sister was married to somebody in or near Kamarpukur. He was a young boy then. One day he went with his sister and her husband by bullock cart. They stopped at the Haldarpukur pond when the boy became thirsty. The boy went to the lake alone. Sri Ramakrishna was standing by a tree, holding a branch. The boy did not know how to drink the water without a cup. Sri Ramakrishna cupped his hands and told him, 'Now you drink.' And he talked with the boy. He told him to think of him whenever he was in difficulty. After a while the sister came running and snatched the boy away from Sri Ramakrishna, who was known by the villagers as 'Mad Gadai.'

"The boy forgot the whole episode. Much later in life, he had

---

* See Swami Chetanananda's *Sri Ramakrishna and His Divine Play*, a retranslation of *Sri Ramakrishna: The Great Master*, by Swami Saradananda (IV.3.19): Sri Ramakrishna described his vision at Manikarnika ghat, Banaras: "I saw a tall white figure with tawny matted hair steadily approach each funeral pyre in turn, carefully raise each individual soul from its cast-off body, and whisper into its ear the particular name of Brahman that liberates a soul. Seated on the opposite side of the pyre, the all-powerful Divine Mother Kali untied the gross, subtle, and causal knots of bondage created by each individual soul, thus sending the soul to the Absolute by opening the gate of liberation. Lord Vishwanath was blessing those souls by bestowing in an instant the experience of nondual, infinite bliss that people can attain only after ages of concentration and austerity."

some troubles. Whenever he thought of that 'Mad Gadai,' Thakur appeared to him, and his problems were solved. Only afterward did he learn that Sri Ramakrishna and that 'Mad Gadai' were one and the same. In his old age he would sit under a tree most of the time and chant 'Jaya Sri Ramakrishna.'"

Swami Prabhavananda told how Binodini, the famous actress in Girish Ghosh's theater, came to see Sri Ramakrishna during his last illness. She was disguised as an English boy and was let in to see him. Atul, Girish's brother, brought her. When she took her hat off, her hair fell over her shoulders. Thakur laughed. He put his foot on her heart and went into samadhi. (9/27/1973)

"Ramlal, the nephew of Sri Ramakrishna, came to take care of Thakur. Ramlal was from a village. When he saw so many carriages bringing visitors to Thakur, he was astounded and said, 'Uncle, what is all this that you have done?'

"Thakur answered with a Bengali proverb: The widow says, 'My husband died early in the evening; I have the whole night to weep.' The meaning is, 'You have only seen this much. Wait, wait; you will see much more!'" (6/12/1974)

"Sri Ramakrishna is an incarnation of the Primal Energy [Shakti] —Swami Shivananda said that. Sri Ramakrishna said about his own coming: 'This time the source is stirred.' And don't you remember that when he passed away, Holy Mother said, 'Mother why are you leaving me?'"

"With the coming of Sri Ramakrishna the *kundalini* [spiritual energy] of the universe is awakened." Swami Prabhavananda added that through Sri Ramakrishna's advent it is easier for anyone in this age to realize God, no matter who his chosen ideal is. He does not have to worship Sri Ramakrishna. (10/1962)

Tonight a disciple asked Swami Prabhavananda how to reconcile two views of Sri Ramakrishna: first, that he is an avatar of Vishnu* ("He who was Rama and he who was Krishna is born as

* See *Sri Ramakrishna: The Great Master*, II.8.25.

Ramakrishna"), and second, the view that he is an incarnation of the Primal Energy.

Swami said, "We just don't know. Accept him as everything." Then Swami quoted a line in Bengali, extolling Sri Ramakrishna as the source of all avatars. (6/5/1963)

"Swami Vijnanananda said that the Ramakrishna loka [realm] is here. Right in your own heart is the presence of God. And in him you find everybody." (1/26/1963)

"The universality and harmony which Sri Ramakrishna lived in his life has been accomplished by him. The vibrations are in the atmosphere. They must manifest."

"Once Swami Turiyananda was asked, 'You and Swamiji have received nirvikalpa samadhi. What is the difference between you?' Swami Turiyananda answered, 'There is no difference in that experience; but Thakur made him great.'

"On another occasion, Swami Turiyananda said, 'Swamiji is like an ocean liner. He can take many across the ocean of this world. I am like a rowboat; I can take only a few.'"

Swami Ambikananda, a senior disciple of Swami Brahmananda, sent Swami Prabhavananda the following story. Swami said that it shows Swami Vivekananda in the paramahamsa mood [to be both in divine ecstasy and actively wakeful]:

"Swamiji was walking on the Belur Math grounds, smoking a hookah, dressed only in a kaupin, hat, and boots. He was walking up and down, saying to himself in Sanskrit, 'To be egotistic is like being drunk. To be glorified is hell. And to be famous is like the filth of a pig.'"

Swami Brahmananda told Swami that one day Swami Vivekananda, he, and several other brother-disciples were seated on the western verandah of Belur Math. Suddenly Swamiji said to Maharaj, "Raja, don't you see Brahman? Brahman is everywhere!" Maharaj said that Swamiji's spiritual awareness was so intense that their minds were lifted up immediately, and they saw Brahman everywhere.

Swami Prabhavananda told us that he was present when Maharaj said, "Among us, Naren is the greatest devotee of Thakur."

"Swamiji used to address his letters to Maharaj, 'My one undivided heart.'"

"Swami Premananda said one day that Swamiji told him he had become 'Patita Pavana' [Savior of the Fallen]. When Swami Premananda said this to Maharaj, Maharaj remarked, 'I also have become Patita Pavana.'" (4/21/1976)

Swami Prabhavananda quoted Maharaj: "We saw Swamiji go into samadhi three times, and we saw Thakur go into samadhi so many times a day."*

Swami Shuddhananda, who was an eyewitness, told this story to Swami Prabhavananda:

"At one time, Swamiji gave a course in Sanskrit grammar to a group of young monks at Belur Math. One day, teacher and students became so absorbed in their subject that they forgot to close their class in time for the vesper service. When none of the monks came into the shrine room, Swami Premananda went to look for them. Finding them with Swamiji, he scolded them and asked them to go and meditate. Swamiji became excited and said, 'Can you worship God only by ringing a bell?' Swami Premananda returned to the shrine room and performed the vesper service alone.

"Later, Swamiji went to the shrine room, prostrated himself, knocked his head repeatedly against the marble floor until blood flowed from his forehead, and asked the Lord's forgiveness."†

---

* However, nobody knows how many times Swami Vivekananda went into samadhi.—Ed.
† This incident shows how deeply convinced Vivekananda was that study is also a form of worship. However, this conviction was also complemented by the fact that Swamiji later felt he might have insulted Ramakrishna by forfeiting vespers for the sake of study in an extraordinary demonstration of remorse, sensitivity, and devotion to his master.—Ed.

Swami Prabhavananda also heard the following story directly from Swami Shuddhananda:

"Swami Shuddhananda once approached Swamiji and asked him for a touch so that he might go into samadhi. Swamiji said tenderly, 'Sudhir, I lost that power because I had to display *rajas* [the principle of activity] while I was in the West. It may come back if I can go to the Himalayas and stay there for some time. Raja [Swami Brahmananda] has that power. Why don't you go to him?' So Swami Shuddhananda went to Maharaj and reported to him what Swamiji had said; and he begged Maharaj to give him that touch. Maharaj replied, 'I have to be in the mood for that. If you happen to come when I am in that mood, it will be all right.'"*

"Swami Shuddhananda was shaven-headed. He was helping with the *Udbodhan* magazine, which Swamiji had founded. One day Swami Shuddhananda made a mistake in reading the proofs. Swamiji said to him, 'I will crack a nut on your shaven head!' Swami Shuddhananda later said, 'Swamiji was original in everything.'"

"Another disciple of Swamiji, Swami Atmananda, once said that if anyone studies Swamiji's lectures carefully, he would find answers there to all spiritual problems."

Shanti [Mrs. Hansbrough] told this incident to Swami Prabhavananda:

"One day in Alameda, some people walked out in the middle of Swamiji's lecture. Evidently he had thrown one of his 'bombs.' Shanti, who had been present, was very sad. 'Swamiji,'

---

* Cf. Swami Nityatmananda's reminiscences in *Pratyakshadarshider Smritipote Swami Vijnanananda*. Suresh Ch. Das and Jyotirmoy Basu Ray, eds., (Fond Printers Private Ltd., Kolkata), 7. One day, on touching Swami Vivekananda's feet in salutation, Swami Vijnanananda recalled: "I received an intense shock; lifting my hand in amazement, Swamiji started laughing. He asked, 'So, Pesan, what happened?' and I answered, 'Sir, it was like an electric shock.' Swamiji replied that almost all of that power had been spent in America. 'It was still more ablaze there,' he explained." (Translated from the Bengali)—Ed.

she said to him afterward, 'you shouldn't talk in such a way as to offend people!'

"But Swamiji was not only incapable of compromising with the truth in order to make it more palatable, he was utterly indifferent to praise and blame. He told Shanti with perfect unconcern, 'Don't you worry; I have emptied entire halls in New York!'"

"When Swamiji spoke at Harvard, someone asked him one day, 'Swami, what do you think about food and breathing?' Swamiji answered, 'I am for both.'"

"Ujjvala [Ida Ansell] quoted Swamiji as saying that he gave his highest teachings here [on the West Coast, during his second trip to the West]. They were almost his last."*

Swami Prabhavananda said, quoting Swamiji, "What we have left here will remain for a thousand years." (12/7/1975)

"The first apostles form a class of their own—whether they are Ramakrishna's or Christ's disciples. The first apostles of an avatar are not mere saints, they are the makers of saints. Do you remember, Maharaj said to a young man, 'If you come back in your next life, you may meet an illumined guru, but not like any of the disciples of Thakur.' This young man was not a disciple." (9/26/1960)

Swami Prabhavananda said that Maharaj came with Sri Krishna. Swamiji was one of the seven rishis; Swami Prabhavananda thought of Swamiji as an incarnation of Shiva. Swamis Niranjanananda and Vijnanananda were with Lord Rama [Swami Vijnanananda was Jambhavan; he was brother with everybody]. Balaram and M. came with Sri Chaitanya; Swami Shivananda was with Buddha; Swamis Ramakrishnananda and Saradananda were with Christ. Swami Premananda is regarded as a gopi of Krishna and also as an attendant of the Divine Mother.

---

* Ujjvala was with Swami Vivekananda at Camp Taylor. She was later initiated by Swami Turiyananda.

Swami Yogananda was Arjuna. Swami Abhedananda was with Krishna. Swami Akhandananda himself told Swami Prabhavananda that he was Yasoda, the foster mother of Krishna. Swami Prabhavananda said that Swami Akhandananda had the relationship of uncle with everyone. Girish Ghosh was Bhairav.

"How can any like us claim to understand any of Sri Ramakrishna's disciples? I have known Maharaj, Swami Premananda, Swami Turiyananda, and I have served them and received love from all of them. I can't claim to understand them—brahmajnanis, knowers of Brahman, all of them. But then I would say, who cares to understand? To love them is enough."

DISCIPLE: Swami, wouldn't loving them be understanding them?

SWAMI: Yes, loving gives the power to understand, but then it is according to one's capacity. (7/28/1958)

A disciple asked Swami Prabhavananda if each avatar or chosen ideal had more than one seed word. Swami answered, "Yes." He also said that Maharaj did not always give the *bija* [seed word].

The disciple then asked if it was correct to say that the guru traditionally never gives his own mantra to his disciples. Swami said, "Yes." Swami Prakashananda, Holy Mother's disciple, had told him that. Swami also said that Maharaj gave mantras according to the individual's nature.

"Think of Mother, think of Mother, think of Mother! Think of Thakur, Maharaj, Swamiji! They are living! Nothing else matters." (10/12/1962)

SWAMI: Isn't it funny, the first time I met Holy Mother, she said, "Child, haven't I seen you before?" And the first time I met Maharaj, he said the same thing.

DISCIPLE: Do you suppose they had seen you before—in vision?

SWAMI: It means that I belong to them.

Disciple: That means we belong to them too, doesn't it—even if we aren't always aware of it?

Swami: Sure as anything! Do you think I'll go to heaven without all of you? (10/11/1962)

Disciple: Swami, if you have given us the name of the Lord, does that mean he has accepted our karmas?

Swami: Yes.

Swami: This I can guarantee: At the moment of death you will have the vision of the Lord. You will get it because you are initiated. It is the power of God that works.

Disciple: Can't it happen before death?

Swami: Yes, but you have to work for that. (The night before Shiva Ratri, 2/17/1966)

Disciple: Swami, if you should go away on a trip, or if you should die before I do, would you come back if I go through a spiritual crisis and need you?

Swami laughs.

Disciple: Why are you laughing?

Swami: Oh, I just feel like laughing.

Then Swami said very seriously, "Guru is within."

Disciple: Swami, do you want pears or apples for dessert?

Swami: Oh, I have the four fruits—dharma, artha, kama, and moksha [righteousness, wealth, legitimate desire, and liberation], through Maharaj's grace.

Disciple: How about giving us some of those fruits?

Swami: I didn't get them just for myself.

"The Lord needs his devotees, and the devotees need the Lord. In the same way—I need you, and you need me. And even if I am no longer here, I will still be with you." (Swami on his 72nd birthday, at the end of his birthday reception)

CHAPTER THIRTEEN

Spiritual Practice and Renunciation

"Our position is: You sacrifice yourself for your family.
"You sacrifice your family for your country.
"You sacrifice your country for mankind. You sacrifice everything for God."
Swami Prabhavananda explained that by serving God we serve mankind. (5/1966)

"We must be a sacrifice at the altar of God and of mankind—for the good of many, for the happiness of many."

"Freedom is the watchword for growth. Without freedom there can be no growth." (10/1957)

"Maharaj said, 'Our life together is bound by love—not by rules and regulations.'"

"One day Swami Dhirananda came to Maharaj and said, 'Maharaj, we need more rules.'
   MAHARAJ: Didn't Swamiji make some rules?
   Dhirananda: Yes, Maharaj, but we need more rules.
   Then Maharaj remarked: "Krishnalal, we don't need more rules; we need more love!"

"If forced disciplines could produce saints, the Catholic orders could produce graduate saints every year. I don't know of any discipline except love. Love the guru, meditate! Chant the name of the Lord! The guru is one with God.

"I lived with those disciples of Thakur. They did not give us any disciplines; they gave us love. If I have to make rules and regulations, I have to get them from books." (7/30/1961)

"I don't believe in renunciation; I believe in loving the Lord." (11/1952)

"Our life means control of our impulses—especially for self-gratification. It is natural that we all have impulses, but we have to control them. It is self-discipline. There is one principle: forget yourself. If you have that one principle in mind, you will know what to do and what not to do." (11/1961)

DISCIPLE: Swami, if we can't renounce in thought and word what we renounce in deed—if we can't make thought, word, and deed one, as Sri Ramakrishna said we should—are we hypocrites?

SWAMI: There is no hypocrisy as long as you struggle.

"Maharaj taught us: Everything belonging to the monastery is sacred. Swami Shivananda said, 'Don't just cut the fruit; take out the thread [the pulp].' Everything has to be done properly—sweeping, cooking, etc. When you sweep, for instance, remember that the Lord walks there."

DISCIPLE: Should one take the initiative in one's work or practice self-surrender and depend on the Lord to open things up for one? Should one apply the idea of "not I, not I, but Thou" here?

SWAMI: You may say, "Lord, give me the power to do your work." Instead of being elated that you have done it, feel that you are the Lord's instrument. As long as you feel you are the doer, so long you have to do your best to work for the Lord. Don't confuse the levels of spiritual attainment. When you come to the stage where your ego is completely merged in the Lord, the Lord will take all duties away from you; someone else will do your work. It is not possible to work without ego. Even when Christ and Sri Ramakrishna preached, they had to have ego; but that was the ego of Knowledge.

Disciple: At the beginning and at the end of work, I try to remember to say, "May all actions be offered to you as worship, Lord." Still, I don't seem to do it as worship.

Swami: You don't have to say so many words. Try to feel that within your heart. Your work here is the Lord's work. Everything here is associated with the Lord. You are not doing it for yourself. Keep awareness that it is the Lord's work. Do your work; you don't have to offer it especially.

When you go to the shrine, forget everything except that you are with the Lord. Forget Hollywood, forget Vedanta! But while you are working, make every act an act of worship. I quite agree that we forget the Lord while working or that we are doing his work. But please try to remember again.

Disciple: Are we karma yogis, *bhaktas* [devotees], or are we supposed to develop all four yogas harmoniously? Or does this depend on one's predominating temperament?

Swami: You are to be yogis of all kinds—karma, bhakti, jnana, *raja* [selfless action, devotion, knowledge, and meditation]. Then, of course, there is the predominating character in one or the other person. You have to follow all the yogas: you work, you meditate, you pray and worship, and you analyze and discriminate. That is the ideal of any Ramakrishna monastery. Swamiji pointed that out very distinctly in his rules, that all four yogas must be practiced in the monasteries. We must not be one-sided.

Disciple: You said the other night that one should have a relationship with the Lord as father, or friend, or servant, etc. Does this relationship grow of itself or should one think of it deliberately and develop it?

Swami: It will grow naturally. And also think, "Thou art our loving Mother; thou art our affectionate Father; thou art our true Friend and constant Companion; thou art our only Wealth and our only Wisdom. Thou art our All in All." (1/12/1962)

DISCIPLE: Swami, is there any benefit in trying to develop certain virtues consciously, such as humility or forbearance, or should one center one's mind in God and let the virtues develop naturally as a by-product of the other?

SWAMI: Both are true. Think of the Lord, but also learn that you have to be humble. Make an effort for that. Of course, it comes also as a by-product. We have that prayer:

Be humbler than a blade of grass;
Be patient and forbearing like the tree.
Take no honor to yourself; give honor to all.
Chant unceasingly the name of the Lord.*

Maharaj repeated that verse many times to me. (1/12/1962)

DISCIPLE: We have come here to know God, and yet what I have come to know are all these other things—like my mind, my faults, and weaknesses.

SWAMI: Ordinarily a man does not realize what the nature of his mind is. He fulfills any impulse. He does not analyze at all. He is like a dry leaf at the mercy of the wind. But if you take to spiritual life and you try to meditate intensely, you learn about the nature of the rascal mind. A monk or nun's life is like a white cloth. You learn how strong your passions are. On a dirty cloth, a little more dirt doesn't show. When you become aware of these passions, pray fervently, "Lord, help me! Free me from lust and other passions."

Referring to the atmosphere of our Vedanta centers, Swami said, "We are really living in a different world—all the three places [Hollywood, Santa Barbara, Trabuco Canyon]."

DISCIPLE: Someone mentioned that since we live in the Lord's place we don't feel the atmosphere as much as we did before, and, moreover, that we seemed to struggle harder to meditate than when we lived on the outside.

* A verse from "The Eight Teachings of Sri Chaitanya," which is daily chanted after morning meditation at the Vedanta Society of Southern California.

Swami: You are going through it, and so you don't feel anything. It takes time. Have patience and perseverance.

Disciple: We sometimes get discouraged, but I guess we mustn't.

Swami: What good does it do to get discouraged? Anyway, you have nothing else to do. As Swamiji said, "Suppose we don't realize Rama, shall we worship Shyama [if we don't realize God, should we then embrace the world]?"

Swami [to a disciple]: You know, I feel the pulse of this place. I also feel the pulse of each individual. I know whether you are thinking the right way or not. I know when your minds are disturbed.

Disciple: It must be very hard on you to know all that.

Swami: Yes, it is hard. (3/11/1961)

"There is a teaching of Maharaj which is very helpful. Feel that unless you think of God you will be crushed to pieces. If you can bring that feeling, it does work." (2/9/1962)

A question about obstacles in spiritual life was asked.

Swami: Obstacles are of different kinds. They are either from past karmas, or the devas may get jealous of someone's spiritual progress ... Your mind may feel devoted, and suddenly lust arises.

Swami mentioned that when X was on purascharana, she told him one day that she simply couldn't make japa. Swami asked her to do the worship. He said, as he had told us many times before, that the ritual worship is very efficacious for overcoming such obstacles. (1/12/1962)

Disciple: Swami, did you say in the Thursday class that the gopis were always conscious that Krishna was God? Did I ever hear you say, or read somewhere, that they were not conscious of his divinity, and that if one loves an Incarnation one doesn't have to be aware that he is God?

Swami explained that Narada said in his *Bhakti Sutras* that the gopis were always aware of Krishna's divinity, otherwise they would have been prostitutes. Then he referred to a conversation of Swamis Turiyananda and Shivananda, saying, "They said you can realize God if you love anyone as God—your mother, or whoever it may be. But you have to be aware that that person is God. Swami Turiyananda said, 'The only exception is an avatar.'"

"Religion and sex are interrelated in a way because transmuted sex becomes religious power; and religious emotions may go down and become sex."

DISCIPLE: What is real humility?

SWAMI: To be humble is to be divine. Real humility is something you feel inside; it is not expressed much on the outside. You are humble before God, and you don't assert yourself before people. In a group of people, an illumined soul does not assert himself; he doesn't try to show that he is illumined.

To be free from the unripe ego is to be humble. Humility is not slavishness. You know you are nobody; and you also know that you are a child of God. When you become intimate with God, you become humble.

"Sometimes try to feel, 'I am his servant, his maid.' That brings humility. 'I am the dust of his feet, his bondslave.'"

"There were two monks, a guru and a disciple, who lived together. They had a cat. They had no shrine but meditated in the room in which they lived. The cat used to disturb their meditation, so they would put it outside and tie it up. The cat died; and the guru and the disciple died. But the disciple of the disciple had to have a cat to tie up outside or he could not meditate. And so a 'cat-tying sect' started."

DISCIPLE: Swami, if we are supposed to give up desires, should we give up the desire to have spiritual experiences too?

SWAMI: Always expect to see the Lord.

"The Lord is dwelling in you. Learn to dwell in him. The Lord is the Lord of your life, the Ground of our existence."

"Are you children trying to keep recollectedness at other times, not just in the shrine? That is the most important thing in spiritual life. When you are working, walking, going to bed—make japa or feel the Presence within, what Maharaj called *sahaja* yoga [natural yoga]. There will come a time when you are thinking of God most of the time. Simply going to meditate—yes, it does help a little. But this other is very important. Do it frequently! Meditation helps recollectedness, and recollectedness helps meditation. And then convince your mind, He *is*! He is within you. Feel his living presence!

"Pray to him. Think of his attributes. Take the line of a hymn and chant, 'He walks with me, and he talks with me.' Try it! It will come to you. Try to feel that you are his own, that you belong to him."

"Religion is not of the intellect, religion is of the heart. The more you think of the Lord, the more your interest will grow, and there will grow love in your heart. We can only pray for love. But what we can do is to think. We can make the self-struggle to think of him. Make an effort somehow or other to keep your mind in the Lord. I care for no other philosophy, theory, or anything. That is all I know.

"One truth I learnt when I first joined the monastery. Swami Premananda told me, 'Boy, hold on to the pillar. Then you can go round and round, and there is no fear of falling.' And that pillar is God." (2/1962)

DISCIPLE: I can't meditate and make japa at the same time, visualize, and feel the presence of God, and concentrate on the name, etc.

SWAMI: You don't have to do everything at once, visualizing, feeling the Presence, and surrendering yourself. Do each for some time and according to how you feel.

DISCIPLE: Swami, what do you mean by trying to feel the Presence?

SWAMI: When I am here, you know I am here. I may be in my room, and you may be in the kitchen. But you don't keep saying, "Swami is here," although you are conscious that I am here.

DISCIPLE: I thought feeling the Presence was supposed to be a feeling of sweetness in the heart!

SWAMI: That comes much later.

"Try to convince yourselves that the Lord is right there. When I am here, you girls [the nuns] know that I am here, even if you don't come and talk to me. In the same way, think that the Lord is right there. That is the truth! There is only a veil covering the reality. Now pray, 'Lord, take away that veil!'" (1/12/1962)

DISCIPLE: No matter how hard we struggle, Swami, we can't seem to get an intense desire to see God. What is the matter?

SWAMI: Well, you just don't want him—that's all. But you know the nature of God? He is so compassionate that he says, "Oh, I'll just let my child play awhile."

DISCIPLE: Swami, we see in a human relationship between parent and child that not only does the child yearn for and need the parent, but the mother longs for her child also. Can it be the same with God?

SWAMI: Yes! God wants us to love him. In fact, he desires us a hundred times more than we desire him. It's not that he needs us. No, not that. But, you see, the very nature of God is love. And as you come closer to him, you feel that love; you feel that he loves you so much more than you can ever love him. And then you begin to weep.

"As you make the effort to focus your mind on him, he will draw you toward him. As the magnet draws in the object. This is how it happens. And the joy you will have no one can ever take from you. You can make it your habit too to get absorbed in this joy. Then it is that your very existence becomes a blessing to others."

"Try different ways of keeping your mind in the Lord. When you go to bed, think you are prostrating at the feet of Mother. Or think of Mother in your heart. Or think of the Lord seated on the lotus. New ways will come to you. Are you struggling? That is the point."

"You have to analyze your own weaknesses. Analyze whether you have the urge to realize God. Analyze how much time you are spending in good thoughts, in evil thoughts.

"Remember, if you have problems, if your mind is upset—it's neither this nor that; it is that your mind is not in the Lord."

Disciple: Sometimes I am bored with my mantra.

Swami: That is why one is given these different ways of concentrating the mind. Sometimes you can concentrate on the sound of the mantra.

Disciple: Do you have to visualize too?

Swami: Not necessarily.

Disciple: Swami, what is your idea of self-surrender?

Swami: To feel that you belong to him.

"It does not matter how many times you fall. Get up again! In the beginning it seems a struggle. But the moment the mind becomes concentrated and you taste a little of that bliss of God, then you love to think of him, and that surrender comes to you. Then the more you think of God, the more you want to think of him. Then it becomes a struggle to think of other things. That comes through practice and nothing else. Don't stay on the surface. Dive deep! Get into the current, then it will be easy. Yes, it takes time.

"Pray every day for everybody—sometimes even by name. It is a wonderful thing if you do that. It will help you tremendously.

"Do you know what monastic life is? When you learn to be nobody. Complete surrender to the Lord—no 'I,' no 'me,' no 'mine.' You are nobody; the Lord is everything.

"Always keep the ideal high. Don't compromise it. Admit, 'I am still weak; but I must reach the ideal. I have my weakness, but I must struggle.' That should be our attitude. When your ego pops up, don't excuse yourself.

"I don't expect you to be perfect overnight. I don't expect you to be free completely from the sense of ego. But don't lower the ideal. When that unripe ego crops up, well, calm down again. You will fail hundreds of times, I won't mind. But get up hundreds of times again. That way you will win out.

"Run to the Lord for everything. Learn to do that. Depend on him for everything. If you have troubles, if you have worries, come to the Lord—for every little thing. That is the secret.

"We are like an island—a few people keeping a thought current in one direction. And where are everyone else's thoughts going? But I tell you, this island is spreading something." (2/9/1962)

"When you have gathered together in the name of the Lord, there is a greater bond than with your own brothers and sisters. There should be. You must have that respect for one another. You are all devotees of the Lord. If you have that feeling, you will have no trouble.

"I read where Swamiji said the brother-disciple should be regarded the same as the guru, because he has the grace of the guru. You should have seen those brother-disciples [of Rama-krishna]!" (spring 1962)

"The other day I read in Sanskrit, 'A holy man purifies the whole earth.'"

"You are spiritual aspirants, every one of you. You are here to express love. Love everybody, see the good in everybody. A spiritual aspirant sees an ocean of goodness in a little drop of good. What is the principle of brahmacharya? The fly sits on the honey and the filth, and the bee sits only on the honey. Be like the bee and not like the fly.

"Never think of competition! Cooperation! The competitive spirit is in the world. Leave all that aside.

"This noon I prayed to the Lord, 'Lord, I don't want anything for myself. Let everyone who comes here find peace. Let there be harmony!'

"Swamiji said, 'Whatever you do for others is religion; whatever you do for yourself is not religion.' That came to me so strongly this noon. I must not pray for my own spiritual growth; to pray for others is religion.

"We have nothing to fear if we keep our hearts in God. To take complete refuge in God is monastic life. If fear comes—good! Your mind should take more refuge in God. Try it! See if it works or not. You will see, it never fails.

"We are all centered in that temple, in the Lord. The only thing is, we have to keep that awareness.

"If your mind is in God, you won't ever have trouble with personalities. If you forget God, all kinds of trouble arise.

"Sometimes I take my beads and make japa individually for you people when you are in trouble." (1/31/1962)

"When you make japa for someone else, take your beads and say, 'Lord, I am making this japa for X.' Then see X bowing down at the feet of the Lord." (spring 1962)

Swami: Swami Shivananda said to make the prayer for devotion and knowledge constant, day and night.

Never lower the ideal. Do not rationalize when you don't and can't follow it. Recognize your weaknesses and overcome them.

Turn your mind inward; don't externalize it. When you turn it outward, see the chosen ideal in the other person.

Feel the presence of the Lord in your own heart. The highest is to see the presence of God within and everywhere. But do both from the beginning. Try to become indrawn. See the Lord within. Eventually you can meditate on the Lord outside. Our Lord has made it simple and easy.

Disciple: But we find it so hard!

Swami: The karmas—but they also will be wiped out. Through our failings we learn.

You cannot grow spiritually or have peace of mind unless you learn not to criticize others. It is the most difficult and the most important practice in spiritual life. I have seen Maharaj critical, but there was no sting to it.

Disciple: Do you come to a point where you aren't ever annoyed?

Swami: All right, be annoyed; but let it be like a mark on water. I get angry. But I can truthfully say that it is like a mark on water—gone the next moment. If I have spoken harshly to someone, I pray to the Lord, "Oh, Lord, why did you make me do that?"

Disciple: Swami, have you ever been actively hated by anyone?

Swami: Oh, yes, I have had many like that, one after another.

Disciple: But what did you do about it?

Swami: I prayed and prayed and prayed. That is the only way. And it does work. See the Lord in that person. When anyone has tried to hurt me, I have prayed for him. If I cannot forgive and forget, I am to blame.

In this country, people have worshiped me and people have kicked me. And people who have kicked me have come back and bowed down to me.

X kicks me. Naturally I feel hurt for the moment, but, as a spiritual man, I should immediately forgive and forget.

A great saint has said, "If someone speaks ill of you, first see if he is right. If he is right, try to correct yourself. If it is unjust, then forget."

"This place [the Vedanta center] is now on a solid footing because I have borne many things. It is easy to get rid of people. I can get rid of X, or of Y, in five seconds. But that would be destructive. We must be constructive. We must try to integrate everyone." (6/19/1961)

"You have your imperfections and weaknesses. You are here to overcome them. Be sincere! But if you vegetate and don't care, too bad for you! Such a person doesn't last here. As long as you struggle, you are sincere. The moment you give up your struggle, you have failed.

"It is a very simple matter. When you go to meditate, analyze: how much time have you spent thinking of the Lord today? This analysis is to show you, 'I have not done enough.' Pray to the Lord, 'May I keep my mind in you!'" (10/26/1960)

"If you want to be happy, never hold an ill thought against anyone. Never feel it is 'righteous indignation.' If you are irritated with someone, think of the Lord in that person blessing him. Think of Mother in his heart blessing him. Not 'Lord, help me to overcome this!' Think of the Lord in him. Bring a positive thought of love; otherwise each one reacts, and there will be parties pulling against one another. The whole atmosphere of the place will be poisoned. Forgive, forgive—that is the life of a spiritual aspirant. Consider sometimes, 'It is a blessing that my ego is hurt.' It makes us humble. That is austerity. That is discipline in spiritual life. Hatred does not conquer hatred. Love alone conquers hatred. Conquer everyone by your love. Practice this even for three days, and you will see the results. Let these truths not be confined only to books."

Disciple: Swami, doesn't this love come after you have love for God?

Swami: No, you have to start with love and sympathy for people. It is no good to sit back and say, "Let me wait till I have love for the Lord, then I will have that universal love." Pray, pray, pray! Have love and sympathy for all.

Disciple: Swami, the trouble is that if someone hates us or resents us, we have the reaction of wanting to protect ourselves, even though we know it is a human thing to do and we should depend on the Lord.

Swami: Don't protect yourself. You ruin yourself that way! You are all here to overcome your human nature and to become divine. Pray to the Lord for protection—not against that person, but, "Please protect me; make me fearless." Approach the Lord for everything.

Don't you know the story of Lord Shiva and Parvati? They were sitting together, chatting, when suddenly Lord Shiva got up and left. After a couple of minutes he returned, so Parvati asked him where he had been.

"You see," said Lord Shiva, "one of my devotees was attacked by some robbers and prayed to me for help. But when I reached him, I found he was already chasing the robbers away with a stick. He didn't need me. So I came back again."

How to see God in a wicked person? Don't try to see God in the character of the man. The wickedness is not God. Behind the character, behind the name and form, is the presence of God.

You cannot change the world. Pray for everybody. But by praying for everybody, you help yourself. Transform yourself. Don't dwell on what such and such a person is doing, or what he is thinking of you. Rise above these things by thinking of the Lord. Learn to fix a part of your mind upon God all the time.

I have seen in my own life that when someone wants to harm you and you can't do anything, surrender yourself to the Lord, and the whole picture will change. Consider that an opportunity to think of the Lord more and more.

Remember that our Lord is the sanctuary. Practice that attitude, then the mind will go naturally to the Lord. Make a habit of placing a part of the mind in the center of your heart in the presence of the Lord. If you do that, in times of stress the mind will automatically go there. But in order for the mind to do that, you have to make it a habit.

Remember Thakur's story of the tortoise. Its eggs are on the bank. Although the tortoise moves about, its mind is on its eggs. In the same way, keep your mind inward! Practice! If you make that a practice, you can reach the presence of the Lord anytime. (1/12/1962)

"My way is the subterfuge way. I advise you or I scold you. But that doesn't bring about the real change. Then I go and pray to the Lord and ask him to give you a little faith and devotion."

"I hold my children by love. Do you know my love? My love is something not just for one life, but for eternity."